THE LITTLE MAGAZINES

The Little Magazines

A Study of Six Editors

IAN HAMILTON

faber and faber

This edition first published in 2012
by Faber and Faber Ltd
Bloomsbury House, 74–77 Great Russell Street
London WC1B 3DA

Printed by Books on Demand GmbH, Norderstedt

All rights reserved
© The Estate of Ian Hamilton, 1976

The right of Ian Hamilton to be identified as author of this work has been asserted in accordance with Section 77 of the Copyright, Designs and Patents Act 1988

This book is sold subject to the condition that it shall not, by way of trade or otherwise, be lent, resold, hired out or otherwise circulated without the publisher's prior consent in any form of binding or cover other than that in which it is published and without a similar condition including this condition being imposed on the subsequent purchaser

A CIP record for this book is available from the British Library

ISBN 978–0–571–28782–6

Contents

	Author's Preface	7
1	Divine Afflatus	11
2	Poetry in Porkopolis	44
3	The Straight and Narrow	67
4	The Billhook	81
5	Family Feuds	99
6	Style of Despair	125
	Index	*147*

Preface

Why 'little magazines'? No one has ever quite been sure where the term came from (though *The Little Review* has been suggested as a probable source) and it is not easy to define what credentials a magazine requires in order to fit into the genre. There have been large magazines with tiny circulations and there have been diminutive sheets which have reached thousands of readers. But all 'little magazines' have been small in one or another of these ways, and usually in both. They have had small resources, small respect for the supposed mysteries of 'how to run a business', small appeal outside a very small minority of readers.

And yet most of them have had arrestingly large-scale ambitions, a deep sense of the unique importance of their task. They have usually felt that they were making points, supporting gifts, promoting tendencies which would otherwise have been fatally neglected. They have seen themselves as nurturing literary growth at a level subtler and more crucial than could ever be imagined by the commercial or 'established' press. And here perhaps one can hazard a definition that will cover most of the whole field. The little magazine is one which exists, indeed thrives, outside the usual business structure of magazine production and distribution; it is independent, amateur and idealistic – it doesn't (or, shall we say, feels that it shouldn't) need to print anything it doesn't want to print.

There have been literally thousands of magazines this century which could be said to fit with this broad definition. Most of them have been rubbishy, short-lived, somewhat ridiculous in their assessment of the merit of their struggle. Many have been conceived merely to push work by their editors or their editors' best friends. Many have served as the revenge instruments of small, disgruntled cliques. At a slightly higher level, there have been many which – lacking real intelligence or taste – have none the less been useful, fleeting contributions to the literary jigsaws of their day. They were worth having at the time, but are today pretty well indistinguishable from one another: period pieces to be thought of – at best – fondly. Higher still there have been publications like Wyndham Lewis's *Blast* or Roger Roughton's surrealist *Contemporary Poetry and Prose* which have simply not lived long enough to seem now more than interesting symptoms.

Early on in thinking about this book, I decided that there would be no point in trying to be panoramic, to provide anything resembling a guide to the terrain. In bare outline, one little magazine is very like another. I felt that if any interesting general points were to emerge about the genre, such points would emerge more efficiently and – it seemed to me – more entertainingly by means of one or two detailed examples. I have therefore chosen half a dozen magazines; three from America and three from England; two each from three distinct literary periods. Each of the magazines discussed here could fairly be said to have made a useful contribution to the literature of its epoch, either by fostering specific writers or movement of writers, or by influencing contemporary taste. Each of the journals I've been taken by has a forceful and original editorial personality behind it, and each lived long enough to test the rigidities of personality against changing conditions. They are not necessarily the best of this century's little magazines but to me they are the most exemplary and memorable. Certainly, it's hard to imagine our literature without them.

In the case of two of my choices, it will be noticed that I have limited my account to the first ten years of the magazine's life. Both *Poetry* (Chicago) and *Partisan Review* are still functioning, but it seems to me that their first ten years were the years of intensity, of struggle and self-examination, years in which each of them was central to its time. Neither has been quite the same since, though both have continued to be valuable in different, less essential ways. One of the points that does seem to be suggested by the histories of all six of my examples is that ten years is the ideal life-span for a little magazine. Within that span, one can discern a pattern. There are the opening years of jaunty, assertive indecision, then a middle period of genuine identity, and after that a kind of level stage in which that identity becomes more and more wan and mechanical. Around this stage, the editorial impulse begins to founder, issues become thinner, more infrequent, political commitments more half-hearted. The editor at this point has to make a choice: to stop altogether, or to allow his journal to slip into a faceless survival. Most stop, and those which don't never quite manage to recapture the excitements of their youth. It is in the nature of the little magazine that it should believe that no one else could do what it is doing. This belief is almost always tied to the requirements of a particular period, to a particular set of literary rights or wrongs. It can rarely be carried forward to confront subsequent periods, subsequent challenges. Each magazine needs a new decade, and each decade needs a new magazine.

1

Divine Afflatus

I was now twenty-one. And I felt it was time to confer upon life that inspiration without which life is meaningless ... I had been curiously depressed all day. In the night I wakened. First precise thought: I know why I'm depressed – nothing inspired is going on. Second: I demand that life be inspired every moment. Third: the only way to guarantee this is to have inspired conversation every moment. Fourth: most people never get as far as conversation; they haven't the stamina and there is no time. Fifth, if I had a magazine I could spend my time filling it up with the best conversation the world had to offer. Sixth: marvellous idea – salvation. Seventh: decision to do it. Deep sleep.

It was in this unpromising spirit – or 'divine afflatus' as she called it – that Margaret Anderson conceived the idea of starting *The Little Review*, a magazine which during its relatively lengthy life was to be in turn perhaps the worst and certainly the best of the large crop of literary periodicals that sprouted in America during the first twenty years of this century.

12 THE LITTLE MAGAZINES

In 1914, Margaret Anderson was an eager, arrogant and rather beautiful girl from the backwoods, enchanted but totally undaunted by the excitements of big city intellectual life. Recently fled from the claustrophobia of her parents' home in Columbus, Indiana, she had arrived in Chicago determined to launch herself into a 'beautiful life' of books, music and ideas. After a book-reviewing stint for *Good Housekeeping*, she had eventually graduated to the post of books editor on a fiercely religious paper ambiguously called the *Continent*. Life was not so beautiful after all.

Hence her inspiration. Announcing it at one of Floyd Dell's literary soirees (occasions regularly attended by such figures as Theodore Dreiser, Sherwood Anderson and J. C. Powys and organized by Dell's wife from motives no less 'inspired', it would appear, than Margaret Anderson's), she rapidly recruited a financial backer. 'I knew that someone would give the money. This is one kind of natural law I always set in operation. Someone would have to. Of course, someone did.' The someone turned out to be DeWitt C. Wing, a none too rich journalist on an agricultural magazine. Dazed, presumably, by Miss Anderson's gushing talk of miracles, he offered to put aside, from his salary, sufficient funds to pay the printing bill and the office rent.

These boring matters dealt with, a date was fixed for publication – March 1914 – and a title was decided on. Margaret Anderson was keen on calling her elevated paper *The Seagull* and A. D. Ficke pessimistically suggested *The March Review*. In the end it was agreed that 'a simple name like *The Little Review* would be better, the little theatre movement being at the moment in violent vogue'. After a trip to New York had netted $450 in advertising revenue, and an office had been found in Chicago's Fine Arts Building, Miss Anderson applied herself to the task of rounding up sufficiently divine contributors.

A minor setback occurred when her admired John Galsworthy, invited to send a message to the magazine, warned her against 'the hothouse air of temples, clubs and coteries'. Didn't he realize (or did he?) that a temple was precisely what this ardent editor was looking for, that Miss Anderson's sense of her own spiritual superiority, and that of her 'marked' friends, was the one editorial principle she could with confidence lay claim to? If he didn't, the first issue of *The Little Review* could have left him in no doubt. 'Life', it proclaimed, 'is a glorious performance ... and close to Life ... is this eager, panting Art who shows us the wonder of the way as we rush along.' The magazine promised a criticism which would be neither carping nor destructive but would strive rather to express 'our perfectly inexpressible enthusiasm'. The editorial ended in a blaze of dizzied rhetoric:

> If you've ever read poetry with a feeling that it was your religion, your very life; if you've ever come suddenly upon the whiteness of a Venus in a dim, deep room; if you've ever felt music replacing your shabby soul with a new one of shining gold; if, in the early morning, you've watched a bird with great white wings fly from the edge of the sea straight up into the rose-coloured sun – if these things have happened to you and continue to happen till you're left quite speechless with the wonder of it all, then you'll understand our hope to bring them nearer to the common experience of the people who read us.

What all this spine-tingling stuff amounted to in actual content was, not surprisingly, absurdly thin and feeble. Galsworthy's sanctimonious send-off message was accompanied by a 'review' by Margaret Anderson of his *The Dark Flower*. Her ecstatic tribute to Galsworthy's 'noble simplicity and noble beauty' entirely set the tone for the other critical contributions. Rupert Brooke, Ethel Sidgwick and Arthur Davison Ficke were the poetic heroes. Nietzsche, Bergson and the Feminists were the dominating intellectual presences. 'The first number betrayed nothing but my adolescence,' confessed Miss Anderson years later. 'What I needed was not a magazine but a club-room where I could have informed disciples twice a week that nature was wonderful, love beautiful and art inspired.'

One can't help wondering how much the money man, DeWitt C. Wing, had to do with shaping the first issues of *The Little Review*. To the opening number he contributed a soggy piece on Ficke's verse play *Faust*, describing it as a 'remarkable Nietzschian drama' and it is likely therefore that he at least smiled on what was perhaps the maddest set of essays to appear in those mad early issues: George Burman Foster's hugely pretentious sermons on Nietzsche. The first of this interminable series of dire meditations appeared in the first issue, and warned loftily of the 'profound unrest' which 'tortures the heart of modern man'. Our culture, Foster lamented, had lost all faith in itself; our civilization was utterly played out. There was only one course of action, and that was to fall with gratitude at the purposeful feet of the prophet Nietzsche: 'Once in the horizon of his power, and you are held there as by magic.' Fair enough, perhaps, the first time round, but Foster was to repeat his apocalyptic message, with minimal elaboration and mounting excitement, in each of the first dozen numbers of *The Little Review*, and sporadically thereafter. Every essay was composed to the same comic formula: beginning with a long groan, Foster would always withhold the identity of the saviour until about two thirds of the way through each piece, and then announce it with an enormous gasp ('And hove now *Friedrich Nietzsche* into sight') and always in italics – as if, each month, he couldn't quite believe his luck.

The Little Review's soft, though somewhat ignorantly soft, spot for the English Georgians could also have stemmed from Wing. In the second issue, he weighed in with some heavy praise for John Masefield, employing much the same terminology as one Llewellyn Jones used to hail Alice Meynell as 'among the stirring events of our present poetical renaissance'. It is unlikely, though, that his influence was really central or that, on points of difference, it could have done much to combat the flood of Margaret Anderson's enthusiasm. In the second issue it is unmistakably her voice that is heard in, say, the anonymous review of *Angel Island* by Inez Haynes Gilmore ('original, profound, flaming, it leaves you with a gasping sense of having swept through the skies') and it is unmistakably her kind of reader that speaks in the new (and from then on depressingly regular) letters section of the magazine; a feature which later, and laughably, came to be called *The Reader Critic*. In Vol. 1 No. 2, over twenty fan letters are reproduced and any one of them could have been written by the editor. Miss Anderson must indeed have thought that she was making contact with her soul-mates:

> I haven't got over your beautiful magazine yet. Don't let anyone keep you from making it a truthful expression of yourself – but you won't.

> I cannot begin to tell you what its pulsating, teeming import meant to me.

It was in the third issue (May 1914) that *The Little Review* showed signs of attaching itself to policies more precise and scandalous than mere enthusiasm. As the issue was going to press, Margaret Anderson attended a lecture by the anarchist Emma Goldman and 'had just time to turn anarchist before the presses closed'. It was as if Nietzsche had visited Chicago and, marvellous, had turned out to be a woman. Though worryingly scornful of religion, Emma Goldman offered otherwise impeccable credentials:

> She has taken her 'heavy, load-bearing spirit' into the wilderness like a camel; become lord of that wilderness, captured freedom for new creating, like the lion; and then *created new values*, said her Yea to life, like the child. Somehow *Zarathustra* kept running through my mind as I listened to her that afternoon.

Miss Anderson's stop-press eulogy appeared in No. 3, and ended with a salute to Goldman as 'the most challenging spirit in America'. The magazine had found a local deity. Unfortunately, though, the editor's self-confessedly 'stimulating remarks' in praise of this notorious subversive proved 'not propitious' for her 'personal destiny'. DeWitt C. Wing liked to keep his philosophies on a strictly abstract plane and, fearing that he would lose his job if seen to be associating with an anarchist publication, withdrew his financial support.

Inconvenienced but unsquashed, Miss Anderson set about fund-raising with the wide-eyed acumen that had already helped her to extort a free piano from the Mason and Hamlin company (she had written a gushing piece in the first issue, preferring the M and H product to the Steinway). Refusing an offer from Amy Lowell to pay the magazine $150 a month in exchange for control of its poetry department, she began begging from her friends and from charmable Chicago businessmen. A diamond ring from Eunice Tietjens and $100 from Frank Lloyd Wright got things going, and Miss Anderson made the most of a series of lunches with likely looking benefactors – some of whom, she has sardonically recorded, 'urged me to talk about my "ideals" and the next day sent a hundred dollars'. A crisis was averted, and the June 1914 issue appeared on schedule.

It was in this issue (Vol. 1 No. 4) that *The Little Review* showed its first signs of an interest in modernist literary developments in Europe. Characteristically, it was the Futurists who attracted the magazine's notice, and characteristically the recognition was shallow and inflamed: 'Started in Milan in the end of the year 1909, the movement has swept the continent and has revolutionized art. Even conservative England feebly echoes the battle cry in the attempts of the Imagists.' (In the same issue, it should be said, conservative England was viewed with rather more tolerance; Rupert Brooke had visited Chicago in 1914 and had bowled everybody over – 'He is, as a very astute young member of our staff suggested, somehow like the sea'). But some sort of start had been made to an adventure which was to prove lengthier and more complicatedly rewarding than Miss Anderson could possibly have imagined. And in the July number, the Imagists were no longer seen as pale shadows of the glamorous Italians (which of course was an absurdly ignorant proposition) but had become a force to be (however dimly) reckoned with. Pound's *Des Imagistes* had just appeared and was reviewed by one Charles Ashleigh (introduced in the same issue as 'Our New Poet'). His piece has comic value as an exercise in the application of Andersonian ecstatics to the icy severities of Pound, H. D. and Aldington. 'Unless a school,' he sighed, 'can prove that it alone has that unnameable wonder which excites us to deepest emotional turmoil, and which we call poetry, it has but little right to isolate itself or to separate its adepts from the bulk of poets.' The Imagists, he concluded, failed to induce this wondrous turmoil and were therefore dismissed as 'restricted and doctrinaire'.

Later, however, in the same issue, Margaret Anderson was more cordial. She reprinted five poems from *Des Imagistes* and exclaimed of them (with no apparent irony): 'Truly these Imagists are enchanting!' (But perhaps she was just in a good mood, for she also announced that the magazine had undergone 'A Change of Price'. The subscription was reduced by one dollar: 'We have paid our bills with what *The Little Review* has earned in its six months of existence . . . we are free of debt . . . we even have money in the bank.') There was no immediate sign, though, in the issues which followed, that *The Little Review* intended to trade in any of its sloppiness for a dose of imagistic discipline. Nietzsche and Emma Goldman still reigned supreme. The new interest in modernism was fumbling and ill-informed. Maxwell Bodenheim, hailed as 'Our Third New Poet' (though he had already been taken up by *Poetry*) announced himself 'an intense admirer of Ezra

Pound's, I worship him', but gave no hint that he was in touch with Pound's ideas. *Blast* was greeted with *London Mercury*-style nervousness: 'Inside there is much food for thought. At least one feels there must be much food for thought, if only one could come near enough to understanding it to think about it.' And in a 'Letter from London', Amy Lowell was allowed to deliver a scathing account of a Rupert Brooke poetry reading ('artificial and precious').

Blast cropped up again in *The Little Review*'s ninth issue, to which Eunice Tietjens contributed the magazine's first extensive treatment of the subject (already notorious in *Poetry*) of free verse. Miss Tietjens took it upon herself to warn against the mode's 'spiritual dangers', and chose Pound himself as the prime exemplar of irresponsibility. It was clear, however, from her somewhat confused assault that what really irritated her about Pound was not his cadences but his vituperative anti-Americanism. His contributions to *Blast*, she contended, demonstrated signs of spiritual and cerebral degeneration in this 'young, self-expatriated American who wails because "that ass, my country, has not employed me"'.

These very tentative first steps towards European modernism were barely noticeable, though, embedded as they were in pages devoted to controversies much dearer to Margaret Anderson's idealistic heart. The magazine was much worried, for example, by its erstwhile hero John Galsworthy's description of England's military foe as 'Prussian supermen of Nietzsche's cult'. *The Little Review* had, of course, taken a staunchly pacifist position on the war, but had never been called upon to square this with its hazy Nietzschianism. Signs that a taxing debate might be demanded of her came in a letter Miss Anderson printed from Edward Shanks. In fierce tones it denounced both Nietzsche and Wagner for encouraging 'the notion that there is a special Teutonic culture which is superior to any other and which deserves to be spread at any cost'. A formidable challenge? Not in the least, as it turned out, for in the very next issue Shanks was on his knees: 'I sinned like a daily journalist and spoke from hearsay — for I confess that I have never been able to read Nietzsche with sufficient attention to gain more than a vague notion of his ideas.'

Nor, one imagines, had Miss Anderson. For her, Nietzsche was the kind of airborne figure whom Chicago parsons would be shocked by; parsons like the one who wrote:

> I earnestly request you to discontinue sending your impertinent publication to my daughter who had the folly of undiscriminating youth to fall into the diabolical snare by joining the ungodly family of your subscribers. As for you, haughty young woman, may the Lord have mercy upon your sinful soul! Have you thought of the tremendous evil that your organ brings into American homes, breaking family ties, killing respect for authorities, sowing venomous seeds of Antichrist-Nietzsche-Foster, lauding such inhuman villains as Wilde and Verlaine, crowning with laurels that blood-thirsty Daughter of Babylon, Emma Goldman, and committing similar atrocities? God hear my prayer and turn your wicked heart to repentance.

Towards the end of the magazine's first year, Margaret Anderson was able to point to this kind of attack with pride; she was achieving something: she was prickling the bigots. *The Little Review*, she boasted, had been denounced as 'uncritical, indiscriminate, juvenile, exuberant, chaotic, amateurish, emotional, tiresomely enthusiastic'. Throughout it all, though, she had continued to treasure the Wildean motto, that the worship of beauty is something entirely too splendid to be sane. 'That is our only attitude.' Or, to put it another way: 'My attitude during this epoch was: Life is just one ecstasy after another.'

And this remained more or less the case throughout the magazine's second year of publication. Imagism continued to gain ground; the first *Some Imagist Poets* was received with puzzled enthusiasm ('the reviewer finds himself wondering if perhaps, after all, this movement is not of most unusual significance'), Margaret Anderson herself discovered links between 'The Piano and Imagism' (her argument turning on the single proposition that music has the same power to 'evoke' images as poetry), and some discussion was provoked by a rambling article by Huntly Carter on 'Poetry versus Imagism' ('an attempt', he asserted, 'to rescue poetry from the lumber heap of verbalism and verbalists, to say nothing of verbiage, and to restore it to the infinite'). Anarchism continued to give the magazine its excited, scandalizing tone. Indeed, it even succeeded in producing a real scandal. Writing of the funeral of an executed anarchist, Miss Anderson put some dangerously leading questions:

> On Thanksgiving Day some five thousand men and women marched in Joe Hillstrom's funeral. Why didn't they march for Joe before he was shot, everybody is asking. Yes, naturally, Why not? Incidentally, why didn't someone shoot the governor of Utah before he could shoot Joe Hill? It might have wakened Capital – *and Labor*. Or why didn't five hundred of the five thousand get Joe Hill out of jail? It could have been done. Or why didn't fifty of the five thousand make a protest that would set the nation gasping.
>
> There are Schmidt and Caplan. Why doesn't someone see to it that they are released. Labor *could* do it. And there are the Chicago garment workers. Why doesn't someone arrange for the beating up of the police squad? That would make a good beginning. Or set fire to some of the factories, or start a convincing sabotage in the shops? Why aren't these things done ... For God's sake, why doesn't someone start a Revolution?

Not surprisingly, a visit from detectives was the immediate upshot of this rousing plea, and although Miss Anderson tells us little in her autobiography of what her visitors had to say, it seems fairly certain that she did not beat them up. Nor were her polemical cries to be quite so specific in the future.

The Little Review's revolutionary posture not only attracted the displeasure of the law; advertisers were becoming nervous of being seen in such fierce company and as a result the magazine was rapidly drifting towards another financial crisis. Miss Anderson's 'beautiful plan' to link The Little Review with the Gotham Book Society (Gotham getting free space to list their books and the magazine receiving a discount on copies sold) failed to solve the problem, and by January 1916 things had got bad enough to prevent publication. A slim double number appeared in February but the situation remained precarious, and it was no doubt partly the pressure from eager creditors that drove Miss Anderson (along with her sister Lois and Lois's two children) out of Chicago to the shores of Lake Bluff. Here she – literally – set up camp for six months, commuting into town to attend to the magazine's affairs. The encampment, as it turned out, attracted just the publicity she needed:

> Reporters heard of us and featured us as a back to nature colony, a Hellenistic revival, a freak art group, a Nietzschean stronghold ... the Tribune made a full page Sunday story of us with photographs of the tents and quotations from my more infuriated repulsions of the reporters.

By April 1916, The Little Review was able to boast two thousand subscribers, and although still not securing anything like the advertizing revenue that it started out with, was at least prosperous enough to offer cash prizes to winners of an announced 'Vers Libre Prize Contest'.

Prosperity aside, however, there were growing signs throughout 1916 that Margaret Anderson was beginning to lose much of her editorial impetus; ecstasy, though still sputteringly in evidence, was clearly running a bit thin. And there was a certain restlessness to be coped with. In June, the Lake Bluff tents were packed up and it was announced that the magazine had taken itself off to San Francisco. Miss Anderson, together with her new assistant editor Jane Heap, rented a house from the sheriff of Mill Valley (the unlucky sheriff was later instructed to keep an eye on a new group of local anarchists and had to confess that they were his lodgers) and there produced one of the most famous, if least substantial, issues of her periodical:

> California was kind to us and we were not particularly kind to it. There had been a certain publicity about our having brought the *LR* to the coast for the summer and the first issue we brought out was awaited with excitement. But maddened by the interest of our conversations and by the lack of interest in the manuscripts that came in, I decided that I would not contribute to the perpetuation of the uninteresting. The only gesture of protest I could think of was to publish an issue of the magazine made up of 64 empty pages, stating that since no art was being produced we would make no attempt to publish any. Jane drew some cartoons of our occupations – Mason and Hamlin, anarchist meetings, horse-back riding, fudge breakfasts and intellectual combats. These filled the first two pages in the centre, and all the other pages were reproachfully blank.

Miss Anderson had already warned her readers that this stringent course might be forced on her, in an editorial which appeared in her August issue. There, she had confessed: 'I am ashamed. I have been realizing the ridiculous tragedy of *The Little Review*. It has been published for over two years without coming near its ideal . . . I wanted Art in *The Little Review*. There has been a little of it, just a very little . . . it is tragic, I tell you.' She had, she said, been obliged to make compromises in every issue of the magazine; this would not happen again.

A likely story. The blank pages (in fact, there were only thirteen of them) made a striking gesture, but most readers probably realized that it derived more from holiday enervation than from any real access of high standards. The 'maddening' conversation of Jane Heap (Miss Heap was an altogether sharper and more rough-tongued figure than her colleague) no doubt encouraged Miss Anderson to adopt her new, loftily severe, tone, but it is likely that both ladies realized that the trouble with *The Little Review* was that it had run out of both ideas and enthusiasm.

The blank issue (September 1916) was followed by a month's silence. Back in Chicago, the editors produced a scrappy issue in November, and then packed their bags again, this time in pursuit of the sophistication of New York. From their new offices they produced the issue of January 1917, and then nothing until March. The March issue, however, promised readers 'a gorgeous surprise' for April. For once (though she could hardly have known it), Margaret Anderson was not over-selling her magazine.

A year earlier, Ezra Pound had made his first appearance in *The Little Review*, contributing a note of complaint about the British import duty on books, and a letter setting out his opinion of the magazine. When it had first appeared, he said, it had seemed to him feeble and antiquated, but he was now able to detect signs of progress (i.e., presumably, of hospitality to Imagism). He wasn't sure, though, 'whether you send me the magazine in order to encourage me in believing that my camp stool by Helicon is to be left free from tacks, or whether the paper is sent to correct me from error'.

Since then, Pound had evidently followed the magazine's progress with much interest. He had been enormously impressed by the 'blank' issue; impressed not only by its appearance of fierce intransigence but also by the opportunity it so enticingly revealed to him – he, after all, knew of first-rate work which could have filled those pages. For two years, Pound had been in touch with the New York lawyer and collector John Quinn, and had received from him bits and pieces of patronage both for himself and for his friends. Quinn had become a convinced fan of Pound's and had made him a standing offer of £150 a year to subsidize any magazine that he should choose to take an interest in. *The Little Review*, which Quinn had already assisted in small ways, was Pound's eventual choice. He wrote to Margaret Anderson, offering his services as foreign editor (the post he already held for *Poetry*):

DEFINITELY then:

I want an 'official organ' (vile phrase). I mean I want a place where I and T. S. Eliot can appear once a month (or once an 'issue') and where Joyce can appear when he likes and where Wyndham Lewis can appear if he comes back from the war.

DEFINITELY a place for our regular appearance and where our friends and readers (what few of them there are) can look with assurance of finding us.

I don't know how much your pages carry. I don't want to swamp you.

I must have a steady place for my best stuff (apart from original poetry, which must go to *Poetry* unless my guarantor is to double his offer. Even so I oughtn't to desert *Poetry* merely because of convenience).

(I have only three quarrels with them: Their idiotic fuss over christianizing all poems they print, their concessions to local pudibundery, and that infamous remark of Whitman's about poets needing an audience.)

By the time Pound's offer arrived, the editors had already made contact with John Quinn. Quinn had taken strongly against Jane Heap – 'a typical Washington Squareite' – but he had just as strongly fallen for Miss Anderson – 'a damned attractive young woman'. And he could not help admiring the pair's courage in having persevered for so long in their dotty enterprise. All in all, he was in sympathy with Pound's choice.

The gorgeous surprise, then, appeared in person in the issue of May 1917. In an editorial announcement, Pound reiterated the points set out in his original letter to Miss Anderson, but most of his space was spent abusing *Poetry* (see p. 56) and lamenting the demise of *Blast*. The reader was left in no doubt that Pound's presence on *The Little Review* would ensure the continuance of *Blast* and the correction of *Poetry*'s sad follies.

And sure enough, Pound transformed the magazine. His first issue carried the first part of Eliot's *Eeldrop and Appleplex, Imaginary Letters* by Wyndham Lewis and his own *Jodinranath Mawhor's Occupation*; his second a group of Yeats poems including 'Wild Swans at Coole', 'A Deep Sworn Vow' and 'Broken Dreams', as well as more work from himself and Lewis. *The Little Review*'s subscribers must have wondered what had hit them. *The Reader Critic* column and Jane Heap's usual jottings were both ousted, and so too were several of the magazine's formerly revered contributors. Maxwell Bodenheim, an erstwhile hero of Miss Anderson's, and an erstwhile admirer of Pound, could not keep a whining note out of his response to *The Little Review*'s new exclusiveness:

> I haven't sufficient belief in the infallibility of Ezra Pound's mind to require no substantiation of his statements. I have several faults to find with his methods of criticizing poetry. He's a bit too easily swayed by his personal emotions, in that regard.

A feebly equivocating footnote from Miss Anderson suggested that she too was a bit rattled by the sudden metamorphosis. She could see that Pound was providing work far superior to anything that she herself had been able to dig up, but she could also see that the magazine was rapidly slipping out of her control. Pound's third issue (Vol. 4 No. 3) carried further lumps of prose from Wyndham Lewis, and four poems (including 'The Hippotamus') from Eliot. His fourth offered seven more Yeats poems, a book review section written entirely by himself (Joyce, Japanese plays and *Prufrock* – 'the book buyer can not do better' – were his subjects) and poems by two of his newer protégés, John Rodker and Iris Barry. Miss Anderson had to capitulate. Anarchism, she had finally decided, had become 'uninteresting'. She could now see that 'only sensibility matters':

> ... after working through unbelievable aridness, *The Little Review* has at last arrived at the place from which I wanted it to start. At last we are printing stuff which is creative and inventive, and, thank heaven, not purely local.

Pound's take-over was complete.

The magazine's readers were not as susceptible as its editors. The protesting letters came in thick and fast. 'An Ezraized *Little Review* will have no appeal to young America', 'I wish you didn't have such a craze for foreigners and self-exiled Americans', 'You used to be very different', 'It's so damned British!' and so on. Such protests were as music now to Miss Anderson's ears; deciding that Art was all, she had also decided that Art was 'What the Public Doesn't Want'. She was fighting the good fight again; and this time she had formidable troops. All it needed was a clash with the authorities and she would be finally convinced that battling for Art was as much fun as battling for Revolution.

The clash – the first of many – came with the sixth issue of Pound's reign. Wyndham Lewis's *Cantleman's Spring Mate* was the offending article. The Post Office seized and burned the entire issue on the grounds of Lewis's obscenity, and thus incurred Miss Anderson's undying wrath. Marttyrdom was obligatory and exciting, but it could also be a dreadful inconvenience. At the time of the suppression, the editors were 'almost literally' bringing out the magazine themselves:

> We hired the cheapest printer in New York, Mr Popovich, whose mother had been poet laureate of Serbia. He had two daughters.
>
> They all took a personal interest in the magazine. We went to their shop in E. 23rd St. and helped with the setting up, to gain time – and lost more time helping the daughters to read Wyndham Lewis. On Sundays to push things along we often took our lunch and spent the whole day in the print shop, correcting type, even folding pages for the binder.
>
> It was a good life except when the United States Post Office decided to suppress and burn the magazine. After our heartbreaking labours it was an affront to learn that four thousand copies had been placed on a (what kind of funeral pyre do they place them on?) and burned to a crisp, all because Wyndham Lewis had written about a man and a girl falling in love.

The suppression of the October 1917 issue came as no surprise to Quinn, who had been worried from the start that *The Little Review* would soon run into trouble – if not for obscenity, then for its still lingering attachment to anarchist and pacifist causes. He wanted a general toning down and saw no sense in inviting trouble for the sake of it. The editors, whose attitude to their patron was distinctly patronizing, took no notice. Margaret Anderson denounced the suppression as 'quite absurdly wrong' and arranged with the equally indignant Pound that he should write a lengthier denunciation in some future issue.

Censorship was the one issue on which Pound did not take Quinn's side in his frequent differences with the lady editors, or 'the two rabbits' as Quinn called them. On other matters, he was always ready to sing the patron's praises. When Miss

Anderson or Jane Heap wrote, as they often did, scornfully of Quinn, he would remind them:

> His name does not spell Tightwad ... He has what he makes month by month, and most of it goes to the arts. I know part of what he does and I know something of how he does it.

Or again:

> Re Quinn, remember. Tis he who hath bought the pictures; tis he who both getteth me an American publisher and smacketh the same with rods; tis he who sendeth me the Spondos Oligos, which is by interpretation the small tribute or spondooliks wherewith I do pay my contributors, WHEREFORE is my heart softened toward the said J.Q. and he in mine eyes can commit nothing heinous.

These reminders were well-deserved. For all his growing irritation with the way *The Little Review* was being run, and with the rude and reckless attitude of its editors, Quinn could see that with Pound thoroughly installed the magazine was now printing better work than any other available literary periodical. For the time being he was stuck with it and had to content himself with the odd discontented outburst. An indication of his ambivalence at this period is that, even while he was grumbling, he was still prepared not only to offer Pound an increase in his subsidy but also spent much time helping Misses Anderson and Heap to organize a circular appeal for funds. At the time when he was most busy with this project, he was waiting to go into hospital for a major operation from which he had a twenty per cent chance of not recovering. A good part of the 'five feverish days' that Quinn spent organizing his affairs before entering hospital was devoted to *Little Review* business. Miss Anderson makes no acknowledgment of this generosity in her account of Quinn's relations with the magazine.

To her, he was a moneyed, interfering philistine who was, if anything, privileged to have a part in her beautiful project. He had to be pacified from time to time – according to Quinn she promised him not to print Pound's attack on the *Cantleman's Spring Mate* judgement – but he more often had to be defied; promise or no promise, she printed Pound's attack. It came out in the March 1918 issue.

In the same issue appeared the first instalment of James Joyce's *Ulysses*. Miss Anderson had received the manuscript from Pound some months earlier with a warning that this, if anything, would land them in censorship difficulties. What more could she ask? 'This is the most beautiful thing we'll ever have, I cried. We'll print it if it's the last effort of our lives.' It almost was. *Ulysses* ran in *The Little Review* for three years, and four times the magazine was burnt. Occasional deletions were made, but always defiantly. For instance, when Joyce's eighth episode provoked a warning from the Post Office Department, Miss Anderson appended a footnote to the ninth: 'To avoid similar interference this month I have ruined Mr Joyce's story by cutting certain passages in which he mentions natural facts known to everyone.' It was just this kind of rejoinder that most infuriated Quinn. He could see that sooner or later the authorities were going to be forced to go beyond mere suppression, and that the chances of Joyce getting his novel published in book form might irredeemably be ruined. He tried, on the one hand, to persuade the editors to restrain their impudence and, on the other, to persuade Joyce to curtail the serialization. The latter course was the one he'd really set his mind on. He had begun negotiations with Huebsch for the book's publication (he had already bought the manuscript from Joyce) but feared that with each new issue of the magazine the deal was going to get more difficult to handle.

With *The Little Review*'s July-August number Quinn's worst fears were handsomely realized. In September 1920 John Sumner, Secretary of the New York Society for the

Prevention of Vice, got a complaint from a New York lawyer whose daughter had received through the post an unsolicited copy of *The Little Review* containing the Gerty MacDowell episode of *Ulysses*. The same complaint had been sent to the District Attorney, so Sumner felt he had no choice but to swear out a warrant against the magazine. Quinn hit the roof. After receiving the editors' 'God damned piss written telegram' he arranged a meeting with them. He described the occasion in a letter to Pound:

> Told them flatly didn't give a damn for *The Little Review*, wouldn't waste two minutes on it, it would serve them damnably right if it were permanently excluded from the mails. They talked of broadening the public. I said 'You will be broadening the matron at Blackwell's Island one of these days, and serve you damn well right.'

At first Quinn said he would not handle the case. Margaret Anderson 'suggested mildly that we would get someone else to fight the case, knowing that no power on earth could have wrested that privilege from him'. And sure enough he took it, though not necessarily from the egotistic motives that Miss Anderson attributes to him. He was interested primarily in trying to protect what little chance remained of getting Joyce published in book form. His first move was to lunch with Sumner and to try to persuade him to do a deal. If no more Joyce were to appear in *The Little Review*, would Sumner try to persuade the D.A. to drop the charges? Sumner, who seems to have been a fairly pliable figure (even Margaret Anderson took to him and believed that it would only have taken a few teas to convert him to her side of the fence), accepted this offer. It was too late, though, for the D.A. to turn back and the case went ahead. Both Margaret Anderson and Jane Heap appeared at the service of the summons and both ignored Quinn's plea to either offer an apology or remain silent. Quinn was far gone in exasperation by this time and made sure that, at the preliminary hearing, his clients would have no chance to speak. Nonetheless *The Little Review* turned out in force:

> There was Heep (*sic*) plus Anderson, and plus heaps of other Heeps and Andersons. Some goodlooking and some indifferent. The two rows of them looking as though a fashionable whore house had been pinched and all its inmates haled into court, with Heep in the part of the brazen madame.

Quinn tried hard to get the case thrown out at this early stage, adopting the handily philistine position that the work couldn't be incomprehensible and corrupting at the same time, but the judge – though, according to Quinn, he had thoroughly enjoyed his speech – quoted back at him the passage 'where the man went off in his pants' and that was that. The trial was fixed for Special Sessions and the editors were set free on bail.

In the September-December issue of *The Little Review* Margaret Anderson delivered herself of an 'Obvious Statement (for the millionth time)', dissociating herself from the trial: 'I know practically everything that will be said in court, both by the prosecution and the defense. I disagree with practically everything that will be said by both. *I do not admit the issue is debatable.*' She strongly disapproved of Quinn's handling of the defence, of what she called his 'suave psychology' and his refusal to fight the case on the book's 'literary merit', and during the trial itself – for which Quinn employed much the same arguments as at the preliminary hearing – she and Jane Heap sat in silent anger and frustration: 'Jane longed to get up and explain that if there was anything in the world she feared it was the mind of the young girl'. One can't help sympathizing with them, but one moment of courtroom comedy does suggest that Quinn (for whom it could not have been entirely easy to proclaim 'I myself do not understand *Ulysses* – I think Joyce has carried his method too far in this experiment') could not sensibly have adopted a more idealistic strategy. When it came to the reading of specific passages one of the three presiding judges spotted Miss Anderson in the audience and refused to allow the dreadful stuff to be read in her hearing:

'But she is the publisher,' said John Quinn, smiling.

'I am sure she did not know the significance of what she was publishing' responded the judge, continuing to regard me with tenderness and suffering.

The verdict was Guilty. The two ladies were fined fifty dollars each and an undertaking was given that no further instalments of *Ulysses* would appear in *The Little Review*. Quinn must have left the courthouse feeling thoroughly victorious in defeat.

Throughout 1918 Pound had remained pretty well in control of *The Little Review*. As well as *Ulysses*, he provided more poems by Eliot ('Sweeney Among the Nightingales', 'Whispers of Immortality', 'Dans le Restaurant', 'Mr. Eliot's Sunday Morning Service'), Yeats and himself, continued to foster his young protégés – Iris Barry and John Rodker – and organized special numbers on Henry James and Rémy de Gourmont. But there were signs throughout the year not only of a slight falling off of his involvement but also of somewhat more assertiveness from Misses Anderson and Heap. Vol. 5 No. 2, for instance, was an 'American Number', with work mainly culled from regular *Poetry* contributors. Some of them would have been approved by Pound, but by no means all. In any case, Jane Heap went out of her way to make it clear that he had had nothing to do with the selection: 'I am responsible for this issue. It was made with no compromise to Margaret Anderson and Ezra Pound.' It was not to be seen, she asserted, as a revolt against our 'foreign all-star cast', nor was it 'a return to our former ways', but it *was* American. Margaret Anderson underscored Miss Heap's declaration of independence by appending a note 'to voice my personal protest against the present number'.

In the next issue (July 1918) Pound decided it was time to clarify his position. He had evidently taken disgruntled note of the editors' rebellious rumblings. He listed the achievements of the fourth volume and claimed exclusive credit for them. But a man can't live on credit:

> My net value to the concern appears to be about $2350; of which over $2000 does not 'accrue' to the protagonist. It might be argued with some subtlety that I make the limited public an annual present of that sum, for the privilege of giving them what they do not much want and for, let us say, forcing upon them a certain amount of literature, and a certain amount of enlightened criticism. This donation I have willingly made, and will as willingly repeat, *but* I can not be expected to keep it up for an indefinite period.

Warming to his indignation, he made it clear that if *The Little Review* didn't soon start paying at least his board and rent, he would have to take drastic action:

> It is bad economy for me to spend a morning tying up stray copies of *The Little Review* for posting, or in answering queries as to why last month's number hasn't arrived. This function could be carried on by a deputy, almost by an infant . . .

> Roughly speaking; either *The Little Review* will have to provide me with the necessities of life and a reasonable amount of leisure by May 1st 1919, or I shall have to apply my energies elsewhere.

In the September issue Pound was mysteriously named as London Editor instead of Foreign Editor, and the only response to his ultimatum was from a reader who regretted that 'We cannot make any helpful suggestions to Ezra about the rent, but he can solve his board by eating the goose he has cooked for himself'. In the same issue, Pound managed a further thrust at Jane Heap's awakening Americanism by printing an article on 'The Western School' by Edgar Jepson. The article, which mounted a pretty savage attack on Vachel Lindsay, Lee Masters, Robert Frost ('a maundering dribble') and other *Poetry* favourites, was reprinted from the *English Review*. It had, Pound hinted, originally been commissioned by *Poetry* 'and then rejected for its lack of flattery, its lack of kow-tow to certain local celebrities'. Jepson singled out Eliot as the only American poet worth bothering about. Harriet Monroe retaliated in the November issue; the article, she said, had been rejected merely for its 'cheap incompetence'. But Pound was no doubt well pleased with having delivered simultaneously a slap at Miss Monroe and at *The Little Review*'s own heretical tendencies, and also with having contrived a handsome plug for T. S. Eliot. (It has been noted that William Carlos Williams's *Kora In Hell* had its origins in his anger at Jepson's promotion of Eliot as a great American.)

Jane Heap was clearly well aware of what Pound was up to. In Harriet Monroe's protest (which was reprinted from *Poetry*) there had been a passing sneer at Pound's 'dictatorship' of *The Little Review*. Taking this up, Miss Heap set about clarifying *her* position:

> We have let Ezra Pound be our foreign editor in the only way we see it. We have let him be as foreign as he likes: foreign to taste, foreign to courtesy, foreign to our standards of Art. All because we believe in the fundamental idea back of our connection with Mr Pound: the interest and value of an intellectual communication between Europe and America.

That 'foreign to our standards of Art' was a distinctly new note and one wonders if Margaret Anderson was given a chance to protest against the plural. Jane Heap went on, with mounting vigour, to denounce the Jepson article – 'Cursing, endless repetitions of abuse of all outsiders, and a mutual self-advertising agency for themselves, seem to be a popular kind of indoor sport of the literary lizards in London. They call it criticism' – and to take a passing swipe at the Henry James number. This issue had been, at least in part, Quinn's brainchild and it was no accident that Miss Heap refered to its 'legal smell: "Step into my office and I will tell you of Mr James."' The climax of her tirade came with her rejoinder to Pound's anti-Americanism. His

> animadversions of his own countrymen induce a sullen boredom and a greater inattention of the arts, while his 'slurs' and 'insults' of foreign races and nationalities living here arouse anger and bewilderment ... there are some of us who come from races of ancient culture to whom Mr Pound's ravings sound but the torturings of an inferiority complex.

And, as if all this weren't enough, Miss Heap also confessed herself to have been 'slightly jarred by his manner of asking for alms'.

It was hardly likely, after this onslaught, that Pound would survive, or want to survive, even until his own May 1st deadline; indeed (apart from the Remy de Gourmont number which he had been planning for some time), he more or less relinquished any active interest in the magazine from this point. His reply to Miss Heap appeared in Vol. 6 No. 1, and coincided with his official resignation. John Rodker and Jules Romains (his own nominees) appeared on the masthead as joint Foreign Editors, and Pound delivered a dignified valedictory rebuttal of the charges against him:

> I have been much more drastic in my condemnation of English publicational detestabilia and despicienda than ever I have been in my remarks about America's contemporary or past production ... All I have ever asked of American writers is that they should not in utter and abject intellectual cowardice seek to avoid international standards.

Exit Pound, and exit with him the contributors with whom he had elevated *The Little Review* from flailing eccentricity to a level of creative richness that no other little magazine has ever come near to rivalling. Pound was never really able to penetrate and transform the spirit of *The Little Review* because neither of its editors really understood the value of the free gifts he handed them each month.

Few tears, then, were shed on Pound's departure. Jane Heap, who by this stage seems to have become the dominant figure in the editorial partnership, quickly seized the chance to demonstrate that America could more than match Pound's all-star Europeans. Recognizing that most of the obvious American talents would have to be shared with, or stolen from, *Poetry*, she at once discovered a genius whom she could truly call her own: the extraordinary Baroness Else von Freytag-Loringhoven.

The widow of a German baron who, 'not liking war', had shot himself in 1914, the Baroness had been working in New York for some years as an artist's model. In her spare time she wrote, painted and produced art objects out of tin foil, beads and bits of rubbish found in the street. She also devoted much of her creative energy to the devising of bizarre costumes. Margaret Anderson has recalled her first full-dress meeting with the Baroness:

> She walked slowly but impressively, with authority and a clanking of bracelets. She saluted Jane with a detached How do you Do, but spoke no further and began strolling about the room examining the contents of the bookshelves. She wore a red Scotch plaid suit with a kilt hanging just below the knees, a bolero jacket with sleeves to the elbows and arms covered with a quantity of ten-cent-store bracelets – silver, gilt, bronze, green and yellow. She wore high white spats with a band of decorative furniture braid around the top. Hanging from her bust were two tea-balls from which the nickel had

worn away. On her head was a black velvet tam o'shanter with a feather and several spoons – long ice-cream-soda spoons. She had enormous ear-rings of tarnished silver and on her hands were many rings, on the little finger high peasant buttons filled with shot. Her hair was the color of a bay horse.

What price Ezra's cloak now? The Baroness's work was as madly extravagant as her gear, a high-pitched exclamatory outpouring, superficially full of vitality, profoundly mechanical and empty. But to Misses Anderson and Heap, she was a revelation, a rich and rare embodiment of their own 'Life as a work of art' theorizings. Jane Heap was beginning to take an interest in Dadaism, and it was not long before she was proclaiming the Baroness as the only true American Dadaist. The pages of *The Little Review* were thrown open to this new protégé, and she plunged into them with a thoroughly grotesque fervour:

A-H-H-WHAT ELSE IS LOVE – BUT ELECTRICITY
HY – THE FLAG OF MIRTH AND PASSION AND JOY ON
TOP OF THE TOWER OF THE CASTLE OF JOY!
HAIR – HIS VERMILION HAIR!!!!

The marvellous thing about the Baroness was that, however outrageous her work, she always managed to keep her life one step ahead of it. She appeared at smart cultural receptions with face painted yellow, lips black; with a cancelled postage stamp on her cheek, and a coal scuttle strapped, like a helmet, on her head. When she fell in love with William Carlos Williams and was rejected by him, she shaved her head and lacquered it vermilion. 'Shaving one's head is like having a new love experience,' she cried.

Not all of *The Little Review*'s readers fell for Pound's replacement. When nine pages of the Baroness's wild automatic writing appeared in the September 1919 issue (the work was titled 'MINESELF MINESOUL – AND –

MINE – CAST-IRON LOVER' and was spattered throughout with gasps, prayers and moans), protesting, incredulous letters were received and Jane Heap had to announce: 'We are not limiting ourselves to the seven arts. No one has yet done much about the Art of Madness.' In the November issue the ubiquitous Maxwell Bodenheim, spotting a likely-looking new bandwagon, wrote: 'It is refreshing to see someone claw aside the veils and rush forth howling, vomiting and leaping nakedly', and in December Jane Heap returned to her 'Art of Madness' line and explained:

> In the case of Else von Freytag-Loringhoven I am not talking of mania and disease, of numbed sensibilities . . . hers is a willed state. A woman of brains, of mad beauty and *elegantes wesen*, who has abandoned sanity: left it cold. She has recognized that if one has the guts and the constitution to abandon sanity, one may at all times enjoy an exalted state. Madness is her chosen state of consciousness . . . Else von Freytag works unhampered by sanity.

Difficult to argue with *that*, but the controversy over the Baroness was to drag on for over a year, with almost every issue carrying some new outpouring from her. The first suggestion that Margaret Anderson, at any rate, was beginning to have doubts came with what was perhaps the Baroness's most 'unhampered' contribution – a review, almost entirely incomprehensible, of Williams's *Kora In Hell*. Too lengthy to be limited to one issue, it was serialized, and Miss Anderson noted that her editorial revisions of the piece had been rejected by the author: 'The policy of *The Little Review* has always been: a free stage for the artist. There are moments when I believe this to be an uninteresting policy.' Here is a brief extract from the Baroness's critique:

> Life: sense!
> Art never insults life! loves – caresses ever form-shape who hates – insults life – proves pariah

Thee I call Hamlet of wedding ring – chasing
ghost of honeymoon bliss – to detect who possessed
– killed – once live body
Of circumstance primarily – individually –
insignificant –
since not can blood be filled into
extinct, withered away tissue.

One of the Baroness's more enthusiastic supporters was the new London Editor, John Rodker. Though able to report that 'the melancholy truth forces itself upon one that Mr Pound's worthy band of contributors to last year's *LR* forms all that there is of life in literary England today', he could also claim: 'Paris has had Dada for five years, and we have had Else von Freytag-Loringhoven for quite two years. But great minds think alike and great natural truths force themselves into cognition at vastly separated spots. In Else von Freytag-Loringhoven Paris is mystically united with New York... It is possible that Else von Freytag-Loringhoven is the first Dadaiste in New York and that *The Little Review* has discovered her.'

In 1924 *The Little Review* celebrated its tenth anniversary, and for Margaret Anderson the time seemed to have come to wind things up: 'I argued that it had begun logically with the inarticulateness of a divine afflatus and should end logically with the epoch's supreme articulation – *Ulysses*.' Life with *The Little Review*, she felt, had been like 'a polar expedition'; she was ready to try another kind of life. How much Margaret Anderson's discontent had to do with domestic tensions between herself and Jane Heap, and how much to her (correct, if she had it) intuition that with Pound gone and the Joyce trial over, the magazine would never really be the same again, it's hard to say. Certainly, relations with Jane Heap (herself a touchy, demanding and depressive personality) had for some time been less than perfect:

For a long time I had wanted freedom from household

drudgery, from publishing drudgery. I wanted to escape both by getting a job and supporting *The Little Review*. Jane considered this going over to the enemy. I tried to convince her that temperaments opposed on such fundamental questions as justice and freedom should be opposed to living in the same house. They should live their quite opposed rhythms on opposite sides of the street. Jane agreed but argued that it was the opposition under one roof that gave her an incentive to write. Without opposition life would be insipid – without it she would never write another line for the *LR*. This threat kept me drudging on.

But now the drudging had become intolerable, and when Jane Heap resisted her decision to close down the magazine, Miss Anderson 'didn't know what to do about life – so I did a nervous breakdown that lasted many months'.

The way out of her predicament was eventually shown to her, she says, by meeting Yeats in New York and by hearing from him all the European intellectual gossip. 'I suddenly found the key to my present discontent. It was the time to go to Europe.' A more potent factor, though, in this decision was Miss Anderson's meeting with the singer Georgette Leblanc. Bowled over by Leblanc (her 'mysterious, beautiful and theatrical face'), she made plans to go with her on a forthcoming European tour, serving (she hoped) as her accompanist. After spending two musical months with her in New Jersey (months in which she met George Antheil, Pound's future protegé, practised the piano all day and took part in private concerts every evening), Miss Anderson was ready to put her case more firmly to Jane Heap than she had been able to before:

> I am definitely giving up *The Little Review*, I told Jane.
> You can't give it up. You started it.
> Are you mad? I started it – I can give it up.
> You have no sense of responsibility.

Self-preservation is the first responsibility.
You certainly can't give it up.
I certainly can give it up. I'll give it to you.

And so Margaret Anderson left for Europe. From this point on, the magazine was to serve as a fairly random repository for continental modernists – Cocteau, Tzara and Brancusi were among the favourites – and its interest shifted, in Margaret Anderson's absence, from literature to painting and sculpture. Special numbers began to appear more frequently than orthodox numbers – a sure sign of waning editorial impulse. One issue served as a catalogue to a theatre exhibition organized by Jane Heap. Even the brief restoration of Ezra Pound as a member of the magazine's staff failed to restore a sense of direction, and from 1923 (the year of Margaret Anderson's departure, and a year in which no issues were published) until its eventual demise, it was clearly just a matter of time before Jane succumbed to her colleague's discontent. Volume 9, covering 1922-24, contained four numbers, Volumes 10 and 11 (1924-26) two numbers each, and the final volume, 1926-29, two also: a total of ten numbers in seven years. *The Little Review* effectively ceased to be a periodical in 1927; one issue appeared in that year, and that was a catalogue for Jane Heap's Machine Age Exposition (Miss Heap had set up a Little Review Gallery after Margaret Anderson's departure and spent at least as much time organizing exhibitions as she spent on the affairs of the magazine). After two years of inactivity, it was agreed that one last issue of the magazine should be produced, from Paris. And so it was. The main body of the issue was given over to a questionnaire in which 'the artists of the world' were asked to reveal 'what they were thinking and feeling about their lives and work'. In some ways, this questionnaire offers a miniature history of the magazine – the questions ('What has been the happiest moment of your life?') superbly Andersonian, and the replies echoing some of the magazine's old conflicts and triumphs: Pound replied, instructing the editors to 'Print what you've got on hand' and added a P.S. 'This refers to MSS. of mine suppressed by you or "jh" ', to which Margaret Anderson retorted: 'Suppressed by me, dear Ezra, and conscientiously thrown into the waste-basket, and a very good thing for you'; Joyce responded with an invitation: 'Can you both please come here for tea on Monday when we can talk over the questionnaire', but eventually decided he could 'find nothing to say'; from the Baroness there was a totally incoherent offering to which was prefixed the following pathetic epitaph:

> This letter was written from Berlin, where the Baroness had gone in 1923 to find ease and the leisure to write. She found poverty and desperation: to keep alive she sold newspapers in the streets. She came to Paris in 1926 where, a few months later, she died tragically and alone.

There were a few scattered gems among the other replies: Marianne Moore, to the question 'Why do you go on living?' answered 'The surrender of life does not seem to be demanded of me', thus eclipsing Edith Sitwell's 'Funerals are so expensive, and oh, the reminiscences!' And Emma Goldman, with scant gratitude for past loyalties, dismissed the whole project as 'really terribly uninteresting . . . what interest would there be to go to the labour and expense of bringing such stuff into *The Little Review*?' A good question, for most of the answers printed display clear signs of strain and reluctance on the part of the contributors; even from this distance in time it is difficult to scrape from them more than the mildest curiosity value. All in all, they effect a properly chaotic closure.

To the same issue, Jane Heap contributed a despondent valedictory appraisal of the magazine's achievement. Few editors can have thrown in the towel with quite such bitterness:

> For years we offered *The Little Review* as a trial track for

racers. We hoped to find artists who could run with the great artists of the past or men who could make new records. But you can't get race-horses from mules. I do not believe that the conditions of our life can produce men who can give us masterpieces. Masterpieces are not made from chaos.

We have given space in *The Little Review* to 23 new systems of art (all now dead) representing 19 countries. In all of this we have not brought forward anything approaching a masterpiece except the *Ulysses* of Mr Joyce. *Ulysses* will have to be the masterpiece of this time.

Perhaps the situation is not so hopeless as I have described it. Perhaps it doesn't matter. Or perhaps it would be more than an intellectual adventure to give up our obsessions about art, hopelessness and little Reviews, and take on pursuits more becoming to human beings.

Looking back on the magazine's record, it is hard to sympathize with Miss Heap's late-won intransigence – like most other things that happened in *The Little Review* it is evidently the product of the day's impulse rather than of anything really thought-out or profound. And yet it is hard also to be as tough on the whole project as she is here. Setting aside the solid achievements of the period in which Pound had the reins, *The Little Review* deserves praise for, at the least, its entertainment value. Frivolous, absurd and simple-minded, it had some kind of buried instinct for the genuine; and fifteen years *is* a long time to sustain any kind of afflatus, however purportedly divine.

2

Poetry in Porkopolis

'A Milton might be living in Chicago today and be unable to find an outlet for his verse.' Harriet Monroe announced this sorry truth to the Chicago *Tribune* over sixty years ago, on the eve of publishing the first issue of *Poetry*. During the course of her long editorship of the magazine (from 1912 until 1935) she may not have been able to come up with any Miltons, but she did provide the outlet – and the outlet is still there today. *Poetry* has turned out to be the most durable of all the little magazines.

If the original stimulus of *The Little Review* was flaming inspiration, it could fairly be said that *Poetry* was born of dogged indignation – indignation on behalf of the neglected bard. Harriet Monroe was involved in fashionable cultural circles in Chicago at the turn of the century, but her chief interest was in verse. And verse could hardly have been less fashionable, in Chicago as in the rest of the United States. It was the poorest of Art's poor relations. 'The minor painter or sculptor,' Miss Monroe recalled, 'was honoured with large annual awards in our great cities, while the minor poet was a joke of the paragraphers, subject to the popular prejudice that his art thrived best on starvation in a garret.' It was to correct this imbalance, rather than to promote a body of work or a critical theory, that *Poetry* was founded: 'An idea occurred to me: the poets needed a magazine, an organ of their own, and I would start one for them!'

On June 23rd 1911 Harriet Monroe arranged a meeting with one Hobart C. Chatfield-Taylor – 'novelist, lover of the arts, man of culture, wealth and social prominence' – to enlist his advice and hopefully his practical support. Hobart turned out to be the perfect choice, and if *Poetry*'s success can be attributed to any single figure, that figure must be him: quite simply (and quite unusually, in the history of little magazines) he laid foundations that would last.

Chatfield-Taylor's simple idea was to get one hundred of his Chicago friends and contacts to donate fifty dollars a year for five years. Five thousand dollars, he predicted, would be sufficient to cover printing and office expenses, and the money from subscriptions could therefore be used to pay contributors. It was very simple, and it worked. Chatfield-Taylor undertook to make the approaches himself and it took him less than a year to raise the cash. By June 1912 Harriet Monroe (who had been spending *her* time in the local library, mugging up all the English and American poetry magazines of the previous five years) was installed in an office and preparing her introductory circular announcing *Poetry* as 'this first effort to encourage the production and appreciation of poetry, as the other arts are encouraged, by endowment'.

If, in her charitable enthusiasm, Miss Monroe had sometimes paused to wonder what she was going to put in her magazine, such worries were offset by one of the first replies her circular provoked. On September 1st, she got a letter from Ezra Pound, whose work she had come across and liked two years earlier in London; it set her pulses racing. The letter spoke, she said, 'with a fresh voice, and promised inestimable value to the magazine, for at that time he was the dynamic center of the keenest young literary group in England'. And also, had she but known it, an indefatigable colonizer of little magazines:

> Are you for American poetry or for poetry? The latter is more important, but it is important that America should boast the former, provided it don't mean a blindness to the art. The glory of any nation is to produce art that can be exported without disgrace to its origin.
>
> I ask because if you do want poetry from other sources than America, I may be able to be of use. I don't think it's any of an artist's business to see whether or not he circulates but I was nevertheless tempted, on the verge of starting a quarterly, and it's a great relief to know that your paper may manage what I had, without financial strength, been about to attempt rather forlornly.
>
> I don't think we need to go to the French extreme of having four prefaces to each poem and eight schools for every dozen of poets, but you must keep an eye on Paris. Anyhow, I hope your ensign is not 'more poetry', but more interesting poetry, and *maestria*!

Pound went on to suggest that he keep Miss Monroe in touch with 'whatever is most dynamic in artistic thought, either here or in Paris'; she accepted instantly, and offered him the post of Foreign Correspondent. By September 21st the pact was sealed – just in time for Pound's name to appear on the mast-head of the first issue, which was dated October 1912. (Some of Miss Monroe's civic self-consciousness can be seen in the rush with which she got this issue out; rumours had been going around that a similar venture was being planned in Boston – but, as she later boasted, *Poetry* appeared 'nearly two months before the laggard Bostonians'.)

Pound not only got his name on the mast-head, but also managed to smuggle in his 'To Whistler, American':

> You and Abe Lincoln from that mass of dolts
> Show us there's chance at least of winning through.

Such sentiments sat oddly with Miss Monroe's other contributions (in the main, stiff, archaic poeticizings from ladies with names like Grace Howard Conkling and Emilia Stuart Lorimer) and also with the drift and tone of her first editorial pronouncement. Pound (though she was ignorant of his views at the time) was to recoil violently from her happy notion that the quality of modern poetry depended in some important measure on the size of its audience. She opens with her expected complaint about the status of the art:

> Poetry alone, of all the fine arts, has been left to shift for herself in a world unaware of its immediate and desperate need of her, a world whose great deeds, whose triumphs over matter, over the wilderness, over racial enmities and distances, require her ever-living voice to give them glory and glamor.

So far, so good, but as the rhetoric mounts, the claims get rather less banal:

> The present venture is a modest effort to give to poetry her own place, her own voice. The popular magazines can afford her but scant courtesy – a Cinderella corner in the ashes – because they seek a large public which is not here, a public which buys them not for their verse but for their stories, pictures, journalism, rarely for their literature, even in prose ...

> We believe that there is a public for poetry, that it will grow, and that as it becomes more numerous and appreciative the work produced in this art will grow in power, in beauty, in significance.

As to criteria, *Poetry* was to be quite unprogrammatic; there would be no commitment to any single style or genre. In short, Miss Monroe breathily concludes:

> We hope to offer our subscribers a place of refuge, a green isle in the sea, where beauty may plant her gardens, and Truth, austere revealer of joy and sorrow, of hidden delights and despairs, may follow her brave quest unafraid.

The immediate response to *Poetry*'s first issue registered enough amused condescension – especially in East Coast quarters – for Miss Monroe to grit her teeth. 'Poetry in Porkopolis', sneered a Philadelphia headline, 'Chicago loves poetry. It uses the proceeds of pork for the promotion of poetry', and the *New York World* rhapsodized as follows:

> From every clime Chicago will draw its poets. Not that it has too few native sons, but the most ambitious and the best shod from every corner of the earth will journey there. The highways need no longer bruise the heel as, fingering lyres, the slender wooers of the muse wend their way Chicagowards.

Rather less amused, though, was the response to Pound's 'mass of dolts' insult. Wrathful correspondents weighed in with a fair dose of patriotic indignation and Harriet Monroe had to rise – she could hardly bring herself to leap – to Pound's defence. She was able to agree with Pound that it was doltish of Americans to ignore their poets, but – and this was a division between them which was there from the start and would grow – she couldn't accept that Americans were uniquely incurable. *Poetry* was first of all an American magazine, and after Harriet Monroe found her feet she was to become less and less nervous of saying so.

In the first few issues, though, it was apparent that Harriet Monroe didn't quite know what kind of poetry she really liked or was looking for. In the second number, Richard Aldington had three mournfully Attic slices of free verse which had been sent in by Pound, but Miss Monroe's own taste seemed, if anything, to be soggily traditional. She printed Lily A. Long's 'Immured', for instance:

> Within this narrow cell that I call 'me'
> I was imprisoned ere the world began
> And all the worlds must run, as first they ran,
> In silver star-dust, ere I shall be free.
> I beat my hands against the walls and find
> It is my breast I beat, O bond and blind!

and this, from Margaret Widdemer:

> I have known great gold Sorrows;
> Majestic Griefs shall serve me watchfully
> Through the slow-pacing morrows.

Such contributions made depressing sense of Miss Monroe's second editorial, entitled 'The Open Door'. In answer to criticisms that *Poetry* could very well turn out to be a 'house of refuge for minor poets' she commented that everyone, even the poet, has to begin somewhere, and went on to reaffirm her determination to keep *Poetry* free of schools and factions. But Pound's presence was already beginning to spread itself; in addition to the Aldington poems, there was a note at the back of issue No. 1 declaring the existence of 'a group of ardent Hellenists who are pursuing interesting experiments in *vers libres*'. It could hardly be contended that Miss Monroe's own contributions had, at this stage, anything remotely experimental or interesting to set against this ardent group.

In *Poetry*'s third issue, Pound had moved even further to the centre of the stage. Not only did he provide five poems by Yeats (including 'Fallen Majesty') but it was made clear that he was beginning to win over *Poetry*'s staff. Alice Corbin Henderson, the assistant editor, gave notice that the magazine was prepared to succumb to the novel possibilities of *vers libre*. It was significant, though, that she was principally anxious to claim the new poetry as an American phenomenon. Whitman was the father of *vers libre*, Poe had influenced Baudelaire. Was it not lamentably typical, she asked, that these American geniuses had been best appreciated in Europe?

> Must we always accept American genius in this roundabout fashion? Have we no true perspective that we applaud mediocrity at home and look abroad for genius, only to find it is of American origin.

Though Pound might well have been scornful of the patriotism, he would not have quarrelled with the main strictures. He, after all, had had to look abroad for *his* American genius to be acknowledged. The editorial, he must have seen, was intended as a clear gesture of goodwill.

In the fourth number of *Poetry*, H.D. made her historic first appearance, signing her poems 'H. D. Imagiste', and Pound contributed a Letter from London entitled 'Status Rerum'. It was the magazine's lengthiest and most lucid statement to date of early Imagist theory, and was to prove a turning point for the magazine. It offered the beginnings of a policy, of an allegiance which had vital possibilities. Not that Pound was beating any drums for London; on the contrary, he found 'Mr Yeats the only poet worthy of serious study' and regarded his contemporaries as 'food, sometimes very good food, for anthologies':

> The important work of the last twenty-five years has been done in Paris . . . there has been some imitation here of their manner and content. Any donkey can imitate a man's manner. There has been little serious consideration of their method. It requires an artist to analyze and apply a method.

Pound went on to pay tribute to Ford Madox Hueffer, and –

incidentally – to indicate for posterity what it has not sufficiently acknowledged: the extent to which Hueffer's critical ideas were an essential influence on Imagism. 'Mr Hueffer believes in an exact rendering of things. He would strip words of all "association" for the sake of getting a precise meaning.' Hueffer's masters were said to be Gautier and Flaubert; his disciples were quite evidently the Imagists, whom Pound describes as 'the youngest school here that has the nerve to call itself a school':

> Space forbids me to set forth the program of the Imagistes at length, but one of their watchwords is Precision, and they are in opposition to the numerous and unassembled writers who busy themselves with dull and interminable effusions, and who seem to think that a man can write long poem before he learns to write a good short one, or even before he learns to produce a single good line.

Harriet Monroe's hospitality to Pound and his protégés may have been developing but there was no real sign that she had begun scrutinizing her own contributors with anything like his kind of astringency. Fulsome ladies were still allowed to get away with their 'eres' and 'yonders', and the critical section of the magazine was slack and bountiful. Edith Wyatt's review of John Masefield's *The Story of a Round House* was fairly typical:

> Wonderful, wonderful it is that in the hearing of our own generation, one great voice after another has called and sung to the world from the midst of the sea mists of England. From the poetry of Swinburne, of Rudyard Kipling, of John Masefield, immortal things still give us dream.

The magazine, like the other magazines Pound was to invade, had been split in two. On the one hand, the editor's own faltering traditionalism; on the other, the seductive energy of Pound's experimentalist unknowns.

Issue No. 6 marks the high point of Pound's influence, and

is perhaps the issue of *Poetry* that has been most remembered and most quoted from. It contains F. S. Flint's note on the history of Imagism, together with his statement of the three golden rules:

1. Direct treatment of the 'thing', whether subjective or objective.
2. To use absolutely no word that does not contribute to the presentation.
3. As regarding rhythm: to compose in sequence of the musical phrase, not in sequence of a metronome.

Flint's contribution was followed by Pound's famous 'A Few Don'ts by an Imagist'. It is significant that Miss Monroe's reaction to what was to be her most historic issue was tentative and slightly baffled. 'It will be seen from these,' she ventured, 'that *Imagism* is not necessarily associated with Hellenic subjects.' She had also not yet sorted out if these new men were to be described as Imagists or Imagistes. It was to turn out to be a distinction that mattered, at any rate to Pound.

Although there had been much talk of Imagism in the magazine, there had not so far been many examples of Imagist poems, and the appearance of Pound's *Contemporania* in the issue of April 1913 provided a bolder representation of the new method than either of the earlier offerings from Aldington and H.D. In the same number, Harriet Monroe printed an article on what she called 'The New Beauty'. It marks her (theoretical) capitulation to the cause of *vers libre*. After a preamble about the need for new forms, she committed herself to the following courageous insight:

> We have printed sonnets, but always with the *arriere pensee* that the sonnet is an exhausted form, whose every possible shade of cadence has been worked out and repeated until there are no more surprises left in it.

Although it seems clear where Miss Monroe got that

'cadence' from, her own exemplar of the New Beauty was not Pound nor any of his London associates, but the Hindu poet Rabindranath Tagore. Tagore had been introduced to Pound by Yeats, who'd called him 'greater than any of us'. Pound immediately ordered Miss Monroe: 'This is *The Scoop*. Reserve space in the next number . . . he has sung Bengal into a nation.' Miss Monroe obeyed, but one doubts if Pound anticipated, or enjoyed, the terms in which she chose to greet his scoop:

> This Hindoo shows us how provincial we are; England and America are little recently annexed corners of the ancient earth, and their poets should peer out over sea walls and race walls and pride walls and learn their own littleness and the bigness of the world.

Such flickers of independence were to sustain Miss Monroe throughout the next two years, years in which Pound's hold over the magazine was such that *Poetry* came to be generally regarded as the chief organ of the New Poetry. She continued to print traditional pieces (this in spite of Pound's rebukes: 'Good God! Isn't there one of them that can write natural speech without copying clichés out of every eighteenth century poet still in the public libraries?'); and she adopted two important home-grown heroes – neither of these especially to Pound's taste. Carl Sandburg's *Chicago* poems and Vachel Lindsay's *General William Booth Enters Into Heaven* each caused a stir in America – not quite on the scale of the *vers libre* debate, but of sufficient vigour to persuade Harriet Monroe that she wasn't just Ezra's handmaiden. Pound's internationalism was all very well, but it never really excited Miss Monroe; she was a patriot, and perpetually on the look-out for some distinctively American retort to her European imports. Here she is, in the issue of October 1913, searching for 'Our Modern Epic'. She had just taken a trip to the Panama Canal:

> One who goes to Panama with eyes not too narrowly

focused must see, in the making of the Canal, the proportions of a great myth. Prometheus the Fire-bringer Ulysses the wanderer, Seigfried the dragon slayer are not more typical of humanity than this modern piercing of the Isthmus . . .

These men on the Isthmus, performing seven thousand labors of Hercules with their giant tools, removing mountains and uniting oceans in a mood of lyric rapture – these men, our strong compatriots, are poets, in imagination and idealistic motive, if not in words.

Will the articulate poets prove worthy of them?

The Great American Poem. Harriet Monroe was a poet herself, or had ambitions to be one, and two issues later she printed a poem of her own called 'The Canal' which opens:

> In lazy laughing Panama –
> O flutter of ribbon twixt the seas!

The gushing expansiveness of both poem and preface was a clear signal of the direction she was moving in – scope, energy, size and American-ness were more, or more explicitly, beginning to attract her. In the same issue as her Panama praises she includes her own ecstatic review of Vachel Lindsay. She prays that 'the prairie muses' would help Lindsay to reveal his 'message, a message which his fellow countrymen would seem to be in need of'. Pound must have known that he could not live with this for very long.

The division between Pound and *Poetry* was to become an open one in 1915. Harriet Monroe had accepted pretty well everything Pound sent her, and although Tagore and Yeats were gifts to be grateful for, there must have been moments when she had her doubts about, say, Richard Aldington. But she suppressed any such misgivings and she was tolerant also of Ezra's repeated attacks on her home-grown favourites. There had been minor skirmishes, but nothing drastic. But sooner or later there had to be an issue which would bring into direct and lasting conflict the essential differences between them. Happily enough, the issue turned out to be T. S. Eliot.

Pound sent Eliot's *Prufrock* to *Poetry* in October 1914. 'I was jolly well right about Eliot' he had written in September. 'He has sent in the best poem I have yet had or seen from an American. PRAY GOD IT BE NOT A SINGLE OR UNIQUE SUCCESS. He has taken it back to get it ready for the press and you shall have it in a few days.' When the poem was ready, Pound wrote again, describing it again as 'The most interesting contribution I've had from an American' and pleading with her to 'Get it *in* soon'. Harriet Monroe's response was less than fulsome; clearly bewildered by the work, she made suggestions for changes – in particular, she thought it went 'off at the end'. For Pound this lukewarm reception was the climax:

> No, most emphatically I will not ask Eliot to write down to any audience whatsoever. I dare say my instinct was right when I volunteered to quit the magazine quietly about a year ago. Neither will I send you Eliot's address in order that he may be insulted.

In January 1915, he was still fuming. The poem had not yet been accepted, and he was having a hard time persuading Miss Monroe that it ought not to 'end on a note of triumph'. Eventually, she capitulated but managed to sustain her non-enthusiasm by taking nearly six months to put *Prufrock* in the magazine. It eventually appeared, after nagging by Pound, in the issue of June 1915. Even then, though, the squabble wasn't over. At the end of the year, Pound was asked to cast his vote for *Poetry*'s annual prize for the best poem of the year: 'I have cabled my vote for Eliot. As you might have known, I see no other possible award of the prize . . . If your committee don't make the award to Eliot, God knows what slough of ignominy they will fall into – reaction, death, silliness!!!!!!'. He must have known, however, that Eliot didn't stand a chance. Vachel Lindsay bagged the first prize and Constance Lindsay Skinner the second. Pound described the awards as 'filthy and disgusting'.

Miss Monroe's own memory of the *Prufrock* episode, as revealed in her autobiography, doesn't quite tally with the correspondence. 'The most exciting of those early introductions,' she recalled, 'after Lindsay and Sandburg, was that of a young Missourian in London, T. S. Eliot, whose 'Love Song of J. Alfred Prufrock,' printed in June 1915, although an extraordinarily finished product to begin with, was his first appearance as a poet'. It is notable, however, that whilst claiming that the poem's first lines 'nearly took our breath away' on first reading, they had done so as an instance of 'modern sophistication dealing with the tag ends of overworldly cosmopolitanism'. Even as a fond memory, *Prufrock* still managed to repel her.

Pound was to continue as *Poetry*'s Foreign Correspondent until 1919, but after the Eliot episode his involvement with the magazine was never again to be exclusive: he had involvements with *Blast* and *The Egoist* in London and, of course, he took over a large part of *The Little Review*, perhaps *Poetry*'s main rival. Harriet Monroe was particularly piqued by this attachment, and with justice – Pound supplied *The Little Review* with the best of Yeats and Eliot, reserving only his own work for *Poetry*. And he was none too tactful about his former allegiance to the magazine. This was Pound's editorial on joining *The Little Review*:

> My connection with *The Little Review* does not imply a severance of my relations with *Poetry* for which I will still remain Foreign Correspondent, and in which my poems will continue to appear until its guarantors revolt.
>
> I would say, however, in justification both of *Poetry* and

myself, that *Poetry* has never been 'the instrument' of my 'radicalism' . . . my voice and vote have always been the vote and voice of a minority.

. . . *Poetry* has done numerous things to which I could never have given my personal sanction and which could not have occurred in any magazine which had constituted itself my 'instrument'. *Poetry* has shown an unflagging courtesy to a lot of old fools and fogies whom I should have told to go to hell toute pleinement and bonnement.

Had *Poetry* been in any sense my 'instrument' I should never have permitted the deletion of certain fine English words from poems where they rang well and soundly. Neither would I have felt it necessary tacitly to comply with the superstition that the Christian religion is indispensable or that it has always existed or that its existence is ubiquitous, or irrevocable, or eternal.

It says a lot for Harriet Monroe's tolerance, or pusillanimity, that Pound was not instantly relieved of his post – and, incidentally, of the small salary that went with it, a salary that Pound had serious need of at that time.

During the war years, an uneasy truce prevailed between Miss Monroe's developing provincialism and Pound's cosmopolitanism – but the combination of Chicagoan local pride with rhetoric about an international renaissance continued to seem unstable and bizarre. During the war, much of Harriet Monroe's energy went into proclaiming the poet's duties and responsibilities: she campaigned from the outset against versified patriotics, against 'war-songs and epics'. She printed Brooke's *War Sonnets* ('the draft we sent him to pay for these sonnets came back with "deceased" scrawled on the envelope') and some of Rosenberg's trench poems ('sent on ragged scraps of dirty paper') but in spite of war poetry competitions and special war numbers, *Poetry* managed little more than a monthly round-up of well-meant ephemera. D. H. Lawrence (his 'Resurrection' appeared in June 1917) wrote her that 'in a real fury I had to write my war poem, because it breaks my heart, this war. I hate, and hate and hate the glib irreverence of some of your contributors'. Perhaps the most apt footnote to these years in which Miss Monroe 'found the war excitement submerging all other interests' can be found in the story she tells of one of her favourite contributors:

> One of the saddest of the war's casualties was Gladys Cromwell. Delicately reared in a wealth-protected New York family, a poet of the finest and most austere sensibility, she and her twin sister volunteered for canteen service in France. But the contrast was too shocking, the nervous strain too severe. They remained at their post heroically to the end, but with release the inevitable collapse came with shattering power. The sisters leaped into the Seine from the ship which was to have taken them home.

For all her evident concern, Miss Monroe cannot hide the genteel, rather bland puzzlement of her response. It was all too far from home. She was more comfortable printing cosy poignancies from the girls who had been left behind. In a single issue of 1918 we find poems by Eloise Robinson, Ruth Gains, Allene Gregory, Louise Ayre Garnett, Antoinette de Coursey Patterson, Julia Wickham Greenwood and Lola Ridge; there are choice blooms to pick from here, but the following coy quatrain can be taken as thoroughly representative:

> O France's lilies are tall with pride
> Flooding the slopes of the western side.
> It comforts me they sway above
> The quiet head of one I love.

In the immediately post-war years, Harriet Monroe's patriotism became more blatant, and more simple-minded. Hymning the centenary of Illinois, she declares that the 'spirit' of Chicago is 'the spirit of active and immediate response to the need of the hour'. It was in this spirit that Chicago had invented the skyscraper and it was also in this spirit '- let me hope - that *Poetry* was founded'. Surveying the magazine's achievements to date, she says that *Poetry* had from the outset been faced with two possible courses: it could have become 'what *The Little Review* is now, the organ of a choice little London group of superintellectualized ultimates and expatriates' or it could have aimed to be 'the organ of a higher and more conscious, concentrated and independent imaginative life of this country'. The first of these courses would, Miss Monroe claimed, have been all too easy to pursue: 'I remember with what cordial kindness a poet in exile once offered to conduct from London our entire prose section.' In fact, of course, *Poetry* had chosen the second, nobler course and its new mission was announced as follows:

> If *Poetry* can help to develop and make articulate the imaginative life of the nation - as when, for example, it wrings out of a poet's over-modest reluctance the beautiful Cheppewa monologues in the present number - then its editors will be more proud than of having introduced the imagists; important as that episode was in the literary history of the period.

This was the first public statement of *Poetry*'s break with the influence of Pound. The Imagist era was over; from now on the magazine would concentrate on what was under its nose. In fact, the announcement coincided with the publication in *The Little Review* of Edgar Jepson's attack on the Americanist trend that *Poetry* had been following in recent issues. The article had been originally commissioned by *Poetry* (said Pound; Miss Monroe denied this) and had eventually appeared in London in *The English Review*. Pound had arranged for *The Little Review* reprint:

> By the reprint Mr Pound freshens up, so to speak, the article's attack on *Poetry*, a magazine which, during the past six years, he has so amicably represented in London. Evidently, this poet obeys the scriptural injunction not to let his right hand know what his left is doing.

It could hardly have been more appropriate that in the following issue (Vol. 13 No. 3) Harriet Monroe should print a poem of her own called 'America'. Slack and cliché-ridden, it celebrates:

> the iron vow of war –
> War to the end, to the death, war to the life
> War of the free, for the free, till the world is freed.

Other poems in the same issue speak of

> Mississippi, you mothered me when the child in me was young

and:

> You, too, America, have seen the hugeness of days
> Break with unguessed being out of the sullen past.

It's as if, with Pound finally out of the picture, Miss Monroe could now relax. Or to use her words (from her review, in the same issue, of Edna St Vincent Millay's book): 'Almost we hear a thrush at dawn, discovering the ever-renewing splendor of the morning.'

By the end of 1919, although *Poetry* continued to print sophisticates like Yeats ('A Prayer for My Daughter' appeared in November) and Stevens, the 'prairie muses' had effectively taken over. One of Miss Monroe's proudest discoveries was a poet called Lew Sarett, who specialized in

Red Indian dialogues and chants. His poems had titles like 'Chief Bear Heart Makes Talk' and lines like

> Ho!
> Hi! Plenty-big talk!
> Ho! Ho! Ho!

Sarett had an immediate impact, and the Red Indian poem became a regular ingredient. One found, in almost every other issue, a 'Hopi Sun Christening' or a 'Little Chief'. 'The wind is wearing mocassins/the wind is wearing mocassins'. It was indeed.

Miss Monroe also discovered a critic; an articulate, if somewhat wild-eyed, spokesman for the Americanist position. Emmanuel Carnevali made his first appearance in January 1920 and appropriately his first major contribution was a review of Pound's *Pavannes and Divisions*. The book itself, Carnevali said, 'has no sadness, no drunkenness, no love, no despair, no whimsicality. No human quality there, nothing but opinions and – an attitude.' As to the Poundian attitude, and in particular his attitude to America, Carnevali strikes an almost Poundian posture of reproof:

> ... we – and I stand together with all the fools he so hopelessly curses – acknowledge that there are many things the matter with us; but we realize that he is not really interested and we consider his talk an intrusion; he irritates us.

There was much in Carnevali of Pound's own fire and intelligence, and he introduced a much-needed toughness of concern into the critical pages of *Poetry*. He was capable, it is true, of letting things get out of hand:

> Enfin, its poetry! Long live Carl Sandburg, to sing the song of his own beauty, and to tell God about Chicago, America, the world.

but he was a good deal more exciting than most of Miss

Monroe's protégés. A Florentine, he had been taken up by *Poetry* on the strength of some 'captivating' poems, but his temperament – it transpired – was somewhat less attractive. He was, according to Miss Monroe, 'the limit of irresponsibility'. Or so she discovered after she made the mistake of hiring him as her assistant editor:

> He accepted with enthusiasm – forever and ever he longed to serve our beloved little magazine. But alas, the result justified my fears. He would slam into the office at chance moments, dash through a few manuscripts with violent contempt, skip all the routine work, and dash out again for more romantic explorations. His six months tenure of office proved the least useful in *Poetry*'s history, and I felt immensely relieved when he gave us up and resigned in favor of a mysterious offer from New York.

In fact, Carnevali never managed to take up the offer. He fell ill with what turned out to be a form of sleeping sickness and lingered on in Chicago in a near-vegetable condition. Eventually, relatives in Italy arranged to take him home. 'He left Chicago, to my unspeakable relief,' Miss Monroe has icily recorded. Carnevali was placed in a sanatorium and was given only a short time to live. But he was still alive, or half-alive, at the outbreak of World War Two; after that, no more was heard of him.

Once Miss Monroe had embarked on her patriotic course, there was no holding her. The proclamations became more and more dewy-eyed:

> I would be willing to put our present day poets (i.e. American poets) man for man or choir for choir, against those of any country in Christendom; because I believe, aided by such small linguistics as I possess, that no other group is doing work so vital and various and beautiful, so true to the locale and to modern life.

This gushingly uncritical note was to become characteristic

of the reviewing pages of *Poetry* in the coming years, and the presence of Yvor Winters as a regular contributor (an exception to the rule) was made all the more incongruous by, say, Charlotte Mew writing about Marion Strobel (her book is 'like an apple tree burdened by an excess of its own beauty') or by Marion Strobel writing about Edna St Vincent Millay: 'If I could only sound a fanfare in words! If I could get up on some high place and blow trumpets, and shout and wave my hands and throw my hat.'

Meanwhile, good poems continued to appear, by Stevens, Williams, Frost and Marianne Moore, and *Poetry* continued to regard itself as a magazine for the rebellious and experimental. But the terms in which Miss Monroe described this kind of attachment revealed how far she was from recapturing the genuine novelties of the Pound era:

> So hail to conquering Youth – even to sacred Infancy in its mother's arms! May the newly risen or newly born solve the riddles and sing the songs of the world!

In October 1922, *Poetry* celebrated its tenth anniversary with a party in its new offices (or office; it was one room in a building owned by the American Bankers' Insurance Company whose president was one of *Poetry*'s guarantors). Poets drank prohibition punch, ate slices of *Poetry*'s ribboned birthday cake, and read their works aloud. Miss Monroe herself delivered an anthology of *Poetry*'s most famous poems – *General William Booth Enters Into Heaven*, *Chicago*, Joyce Kilmer's 'Trees', Rupert Brooke's 'The Soldier' and even some of Pound's *Contemporania*. (The birthday issue of *Poetry* had in fact taken pains to give Pound his proper thanks for having 'with much tumult and shouting turned the dry bones of the past and sounded the tocsin for the future'.) It was a sedate, self-satisfied occasion.

The problem was, though, where would *Poetry* go next? Miss

Monroe was firmly set on her Americanist course, but her efforts to create the appearance of an Americanist movement had all seemed fairly desperate. And her attempt to produce a major American poet had been similarly unsuccessful. Both Sandburg and Lindsay were already well-established and so too was Williams (though there is nothing to suggest that Miss Monroe quite appreciated how Americanist *he* was). She needed someone new, someone Western, someone vast. In March 1923 she reviewed *The Waste Land* alongside Lew Sarett's *The Box of God*. One could hardly wish for a neater summary either of the internal conflict which had distinguished most of *Poetry*'s first decade, or of the dismal outcome of that conflict. Headed 'A Contrast', the review spoke of there being 'two immemorial types . . . the indoor and the outdoor man'. Eliot, she goes on, 'gives us, with consummate distinction, what many an indoor thinker thinks about life today', but

> to the men of science, the inventors, the engineers who are performing today's miracles, the miasma which afflicts Mr Eliot is as remote as a speculative conceit, as futile a fritter of mental confectionary as Lyly's euphemism (*sic*) must have been to Elizabethan sailors. And these men are thinkers too, dreamers of larger dreams than any group of city-closeted artists may evoke out of the circling pipesmoke of their scented talk.

Set against the shrivelled metropolitanism of Eliot, we have Sarett, a poet who would make real sense to those visionary engineers. He offers what Eliot so miserably doesn't: 'the creed of the pioneer, of the explorer, the discoverer, the inventor in whatever field'.

To compound this extraordinary philistinism, Miss Monroe goes on to tell of Sarett how 'last summer, while taking his vacation as a forest ranger of the government, he chased a pair of bandits through Glacier Park for forty-eight hours alone, and single handed brought them back to camp for trial'. Imagine Prufrock pulling off a stunt like that.

The promotion of a mediocre poet like Sarett was a mistake any editor might make, but there was little excuse for promoting him in these terms. And the crude disparagement of Eliot indicates how little Miss Monroe knew about her magazine's achievements or about how the future would estimate them. The simple-mindedness of her poetic pioneerism stood horribly revealed.

Poetry from this point on became what it still is today, a verse-printing periodical with no real policy, no special attachments, no enemies. And this was the magazine, after all, which Miss Monroe had originally set out to edit. Pound's intervention and her own wish to win free of his control had altered its course, but once Pound had gone and once Miss Monroe realized that her Americanist retort did not supply a vital new polemic, *Poetry* was free to settle back into its original Open Door complacency. Apart from a crisis during the Depression, when it did look for a time as if the magazine might have to close, *Poetry* was always financially sound and its position as poetry's friend and shopkeeper is not one to be glibly disparaged. Harriet Monroe, after all, was always more of an entrepreneur than an editor, and as such she deserves high praise. The truth is that, in 1923, she was faced with much the same choice as Margaret Anderson was faced with once it became clear that *The Little Review* had lost its vital spark. She could close it down, or accompany it into respectability. It was an easy choice because for Miss Monroe respectability had never been an enemy.

Harriet Monroe edited *Poetry* until a year before her death in 1935. In her later years she devoted less and less of her time to the magazine, and she threw herself into a series of ambitious foreign journeys. She died, dogged to the last, while attempting to cross the Andes with Norah Rowan Hamilton, the English delegate to the PEN International Congress in Buenos Aires. The altitude, it was said, proved too much for her.

The December 1936 issue of *Poetry* carried a number of tributes from friends, colleagues and contributors. Perhaps the most accurate and heartfelt tribute came from Pound – he writes in effect an obituary both for the doomed, exciting little magazine that *Poetry* might have been and for the worthy, durable 'trade journal' that it actually became:

> The new generation of the 1930s can not measure, offhand, the local situation of 1910. An exclusive editorial policy would not have done the work of an inclusive policy, (however much the inclusiveness may have rankled one and all factions).
>
> It is to Miss Monroe's credit that *Poetry* never degenerated into a factional organ. Her achievement was to set up a trade journal in the best sense of the word.
>
> During the twenty-four years of her editorship perhaps three periodicals made a brilliant record, perhaps five periodicals, but they were all under the sod in the autumn of 1936.

3

The Straight and Narrow

Expounding (in 1926) his 'Idea of a Literary Review', T. S. Eliot warned against the dangers of both the 'narrow' and the 'comprehensive' kinds of periodical. Magazines ought not to devote themselves to promoting the views of a small group; nor should they be miscellanies, sprawlingly inclusive. The proper aim of a literary review should be to 'represent the development of the keenest sensibility and the clearest thought' of its age. It should have an identity of its own but ought not to be sealed off in it. It should range undogmatically but not at the expense of 'critical value'. A cautious, compromising recipe. It is characteristic that, in spite of it, Eliot's own magazine should now be almost solely valuable because of what it tells us about Eliot.

Defining his role as editor of *The Criterion*, Eliot was careful to point out that objectives are not programmes. *The Criterion* had no programme; it could merely be said to represent a 'tendency'. He was content to sound fairly vague about how this tendency might be described. The most he would allow was that it was 'toward something which, for want of a better name, we may call classicism', 'toward a higher and clearer conception of Reason and a more severe and serene control of the emotions by Reason'. One gets the sense from this, as from many other of Eliot's more abstract pronouncements, that the tentativeness has more to do with phrasing than with feeling. In a letter written earlier to Herbert Read, he had been somewhat more distinct and fervent:

> If I say generally that I wish to form a 'phalanx', a hundred voices will forthwith declare that I wish to be a leader, and that my vanity will not allow me to serve, or even to exist on terms of equality with others. If one maintains a cause, one is either a fanatic or a hypocrite, and if one has any definite dogmas, then one is imposing the dogmas upon those who cooperate with one . . . I wish, certainly, to get as homogeneous a group as possible; but I find that homogeneity is in the end undefinable. For the purposes of *The Criterion*, it cannot be reduced to a creed of numbered articles. I do *not* expect everyone to subscribe to all the articles of my own faith, or to read Arnold, Newman, Bradley or Maurras with my eyes. It seems to me that at the present time we need more dogma, and that one ought to have as precise and clear a creed as possible, when one thinks at all.

Although nervous of seeming to impose his own views too autocratically, Eliot at the same time envisaged the ideal contributor to his pages as one who held an 'impersonal loyalty' to 'some faith not antagonistic to my own'. There is barely a single issue of *The Criterion* that could have left anyone in much doubt as to what 'my own' faith consisted of, and few of the magazine's critical contributions could not in one way or another be regarded as acceptably supportive of that faith.

Eliot's defence against accusations of programmatic narrowness would presumably have been that his was not a narrow faith. It was a faith which sought nothing less than to maintain the continuity of culture in an age inhospitable to culture, to keep alive those traditional values which, in past ages, had guaranteed the highest cultural possibilities. It was thus profoundly anti-democratic, profoundly hostile to any liberal-progressive efforts to unseat traditional authority. 'The aristocracy of culture' must be protected against 'the demagogy of science', 'the governors of the people' must be encouraged to sustain 'the conviction of their right to govern'. And, since the artist's role was in jeopardy, it was no longer enough for him to simply be an artist; he must define and protect the conditions in which art might continue to work as an effective civilizing agent. These, very roughly, were the main articles of Eliot's creed. They are familiar enough from his poetry, but *The Criterion* gave him the opportunity to test them out with more discursive and polemical explicitness.

But before going into how this worked out in detail, some facts and dates are necessary. *The Criterion* had a relatively long and secure life; rarely needing to worry much about mere survival, about advertisements and new subscribers. The circulation was throughout unusually small, even by little magazine standards – somewhere around four hundred. It was launched as a quarterly in October 1922, with financial assistance from Viscountess Rothermere, while Eliot was still working in his City bank and therefore 'not in a position to accept a salary'. 'One never knows,' Eliot confided to John Quinn, 'whether any public activity of this sort is worthwhile but it is interesting to make such an attempt at least once in one's life; if it succeeds – as far as anything of the sort can be expected to succeed – it will be of satisfaction to me; meanwhile it is a kind of experience.' As it turned out, during the next two years *The Criterion* was not the kind of experience that Eliot had bargained for. These years, we now know, were black years for Eliot; the strain of coping with his private difficulties as well as with his full-time bank job was immense enough without the added burden of his new magazine. A year after founding *The Criterion*, Eliot came very close to abandoning it. On 12th March 1923 he wrote, again to Quinn:

> I am now in the midst of a terrific crisis. I wish to heaven I had never taken up *The Criterion*. It seemed a good thing, and it is a good thing, but although it is a pity to drop such a promising beginning I may very soon have to drop it and I am quite sincere when I wish I had never undertaken it. It has been an evergrowing responsibility . . . a great *expense* to me and I have not got a penny out of it: there is not enough money to run it and pay me too. I hoped that it would be a solid thing for me, but there is no longer *time* to wait for that. I think the work and worry have taken 10 years off my life. I have sunk the whole of my strength for the past 18 months into this confounded paper, when I ought to have been minding my own business and doing my own writing. The paper has therefore done me more harm than good. The present situation is this: that I must either give up the bank at once and find some work which would take less of my time – thereby sacrificing part of an income every penny of which I need – or else I must give up *The Criterion* before my health crashes and I am no longer able to perform my bank work . . . In order to carry on *The Criterion* I have had to neglect not only the writing I ought to be doing but my private affairs of every description which for some time past I have not had a moment to deal with. I have not even time to go to a dentist or to have my hair cut, and at the same time I see *The Criterion* full of the most glaring defects which I could only avoid by having still more time for it to devour, and at the same time I am simply unfit to take risks which in any case I should not be justified in taking.

Eliot added a postscript: 'I am worn out, I cannot go on.' But he did go on, and for its first three years of life *The Criterion*, for all the stresses it was imposing on its editor, was at least free of economic threat – Lady Rothermere continued to pay up. But not, as it transpired, contentedly. In 1925 the magazine's subsidy was withdrawn; Lady Rothermere had apparently wished not for a heavyweight intellectual journal but, in Eliot's words, for 'a more chic and brilliant *Art and Letters* which might have a fashionable vogue among a wealthy few'. Whatever the reasons, the magazine was now plunged into its first, and only, major financial crisis. This was resolved, according to the publisher Frank Morley – who acted as go-between – in the offices of *The Times Literary Supplement*, then edited by Bruce Richmond:

> 'All right,' said Tom. 'I'm tough. Who pays the bills?'. I don't believe I answered. I was already on the way to find Bruce Richmond. Richmond was the secret agent of the whole thing ... (he) permitted himself one chortle of amusement, then took about ten minutes to list a dozen names which were to be forever anonymous, and another twenty minutes to give me notes to some of them, making a memo that he would attack others. There was nothing for me to do but bank the fund in a separate account at the bank.

The magazine was kept going for a time with the help of these mysterious benefactors (Eliot later named two of them as Charles Whibley and Frederick Scott Oliver), and then in 1926 it was taken over by the firm of Faber and Gwyer, where Eliot had meanwhile started his new career as a publisher. Eliot had felt nervous about involving his employer earlier, and it was at Faber's suggestion that the deal was arranged. (It is notable that Eliot was later to single out the year 1926 as the point at which 'one began slowly to realize that the intellectual and artistic output of the previous seven years had been rather the last efforts of an old world, than the first struggles of a new'.) From that year – although there was to be another whip-round some time after – *The*

Criterion was firmly on its feet. It became *The New Criterion* and ran for a further five issues as a quarterly before changing to a monthly. *The Monthly Criterion* appeared for just over a year, but by June 1928 Eliot had come to the conclusion that 'whatever editorial talent I possessed did not extend to the preparation of a review oftener than four times a year', and reverted to quarterly publication, and to the magazine's original title. *The Criterion* continued as a quarterly until its death in 1939. Seventy-one issues had been published, each of about a hundred pages, and the price had crept up from 3s 6d to 7s 6d.

There were few changes in the planning and scope of the magazine during its seventeen-year life. Essays, short stories and poems usually formed the bulk of it. There was a book review section, small and very selective at first but expanded in later issues. There were regular columns on music, art and broadcasting, and there were valuable round-ups of foreign periodicals. Most important of all the regular features, though, was the editor's own *Commentary*. This elegant, often witty, often hopelessly wrong-headed column first appeared in 1924 and from then on it provided Eliot with the platform, or pulpit, from which he could apply his beliefs to the practical issues of the day. When one reads these 'commentaries' straight through, the obsessive strain is very marked. Whatever the topic, however huge or trivial, it tends to get treated in the same way, and with much the same weight, as grist for Eliot's dark, dogmatic mill.

Browsing, for instance, through a scientific periodical, Eliot finds nothing more deserving of comment than one scientist's passing notion that 'we may look to the isolated as the source of fresh individuality and power, to be paid for in time, however, with the inevitable price of diminished progress'. There is a certain pathos in the editor's lusty response to this banality: 'We do not know what other zoologists say to this, but it looks as if one distinguished authority thought that a uniform civilization . . . was hardly a prospect to be desired.' On another occasion, Eliot announces that he has been reading a magazine called *Youth* (which, even from his respectful description of it, manages to sound somewhat crankily boy-scoutish) and has been cheered to learn of 'the amazing spread of folk dancing throughout Britain'. Straining further, Eliot detects here the influence of Sir James Frazer and finally discovers in the whole phenomenon a 'note of breakers on the reef'. 'This note', he concludes bizarrely, 'is not "the great middle-class liberalism" or the great lower middle-class socialism; it is of authority not democracy, of dogmatism not tolerance, of the extremity and never of the mean.'

Not all of Eliot's 'commentaries' were as amusingly eccentric as these. A brief anthology of his responses to, say, the Spanish War, Fascism, slum clearance, censorship etc., would make fairly sinister reading these days. In 1928, he was writing in fulsome admiration of the British Fascists, and only regretted that a 'nationalist organization should have to go abroad for its name and symbol' (later he was to be cool about Mosley, but only because his party seemed to Eliot lacking in intellectual content and in moral drive). In the same year, he was claiming for Britain the leadership of the cultural Common Market which was one of *The Criterion*'s central ideals during its early years: Britain, he mused, not only provided a bridge between Latin culture and Germanic culture but also 'she is the only member of the European community that has established a genuine empire – that is to say, a world-wide empire as was the Roman empire – not only European but the connection between Europe and the rest of the world'.

There was indeed a strong element of what John Gould Fletcher called 'Hellenic paranoia' in Eliot's careful nurturing of the European idea. Time and again he speaks with edgy vagueness of the need 'to keep the intellectual blood of Europe circulating throughout the whole of Europe', and of course the European solidarity he has in mind would be devotedly supportive of his own special brand of higher than high Toryism, in which 'a doctrine of the relation of the temporal and spiritual in matters of Church and State is essential'. The extreme monarchistic views of Eliot's hero Charles Maurras no doubt sound uglier now than they did then, but even in the middle twenties one would have thought Henry Massis's article 'Defence of the West' (published with some reverence by *The Criterion* in two instalments) might have been found disconcertingly yellow-perilish: 'In order to overcome the dangers that threaten us, we must be able to name them. To put it briefly, they are Bolshevism and Asiaticism. The whole of civilization is reduced to defending itself against this dark barbarism which is so powerfully organized.' There would have been no doubt in Eliot's mind that *The Criterion* reader would know precisely what was meant by 'the *whole* of civilization'.

There is much of this kind of thing throughout *The Criterion* and we can see now that some kind of Fascist ideology was the inevitable upshot of the magazine's aristocratic, Europeanist 'tendency'. But Eliot's right-wing meditations were always more concerned, politically, with the need for an adequate response to the threat of Communism than with any easy cheering-on of the available pro-Fascist groupings. He was fond of depicting himself as a 'political ignoramus' and claimed to be interested only in political *ideas*; political practice he would invariably disdain as necessarily compromised and seedy.

The thirties was not the best of periods in which to nourish high detachment of this order, and as it became increasingly difficult to separate political ideas from their consequences so *The Criterion* became more and more uncertain of what it was up to. The contemptuous anti-bolshevism of its early years could hardly be sustained without adjustments of some kind, and as much as anything else it is the muddle of Eliot's response to the developing seductiveness of Communist ideas that marks the second stage of the magazine's career. On the one hand we can read an analysis of Marxism that employs as its chief premise the view that since Marx was a Jew and since Jews had become 'more and more openly the exploiters of the Western World today', Marx's world revolution merely represented 'the desire of the inferior to revenge himself on the superior (as Nietzsche points out, characteristic of the Judaic psychology'.) On the other – and, to be fair, much more extensively – we are allowed to listen in on Eliot's pondering of what he detects as the 'spiritual appeal' of Communism:

> Communism ... has come as a godsend (so to speak) to those young people who would like to grow up and believe in something. Once they have committed themselves, they must find (if they are honest and really growing) that they have let themselves in for all the troubles that afflict the person who believes in something. They have joined that bitter fraternity which lives on a higher level of doubt; no longer the doubting which is just a play with ideas, on the level of a France or a Gide, but that which is a daily battle.

Eliot has a number of indulgent moments of this kind; extrication is invariably drastic. If the Communists have spiritual appeal, ought we to temper our hostility? Absolutely not.

> The Bolsheviks believe in something which has the equivalent for them to a supernatural sanction; and it is only with a genuine supernatural sanction that we can oppose it.

Much of the muddle derived, of course, from Eliot's recognition that the best of the new young writers in the thirties were responding to sanctions quite opposed to those which he held dear, and that their response was on the whole genuinely idealistic. There is something touching in his efforts to ally himself with them ('we both know what it is to believe in something') whilst deploring every aspect of their creed.

Rather more damaging to *The Criterion* than its confusion about Communism is the complete silence it maintained throughout the thirties about Hitler and developments in Nazi Germany. It was fairly obvious that Eliot would take the clerics' side during the Spanish Civil War – this was for him barely a matter of politics at all. But during the last few years of the magazine's life it must have needed positive effort to avoid discussion of the Nazis. Where references can be found, they are sympathetic, but Eliot himself kept quiet. We can only assume that he viewed Hitler's rise as yet another sign that the magazine's whole programme was being overtaken by events – events which could not have been envisaged (and which a 'political ignoramus' had no duty to envisage) and which *The Criterion* could take no useful part in. Eliot could not for long pretend that Nazism did not exist, but neither could he bring himself to oppose it. The magazine's end was in sight for at least three years before it actually ceased publication. By 1939, Eliot had had enough, and his valediction is utterly dispirited.

> In the present state of public affairs – which has induced in myself a depression of spirits so different from any other experience as to be a new emotion – I no longer feel the enthusiasm necessary to make a literary review what it should be.

He is proud, he says, to have published certain writers and to have done something, however insubstantial, for the cause of European unity, although this cause had come to nothing: 'The "European mind", which one had mistakenly thought might be renewed and fortified, disappeared from view: there were fewer writers in any country who seemed to have anything to say to the intellectual public of another.' So much, and so depressingly, for the magazine's 'best years' (1922 to 1929). But if the magazine's European phase was a failure, its English-political career was, if we are to believe the retrospective Eliot, nothing short of a disaster - although, he would also have us think, a disaster forced upon it by the far greater disaster of the country's drift towards wrong principles:

> In retrospect, it would seem that perhaps I devoted too much of my gossiping attention, as Commentator, to the doctrines of communism. I can only say that I was commenting on ideas or the lack of them, and not engaging in political prophecy. I was concerned with ideas chiefly as they originated in, or penetrated to, England; and the version of fascism, which was offered locally, appeared to have no great intellectual interest - and what is perhaps more important, was not sufficiently adaptable to be grafted onto the stock of Toryism - whereas communism flourished because it grew so easily on the Liberal root.

Perhaps, he muses, it would have been better to have spent less time 'trying to maintain literary standards increasingly repudiated in the modern world' and to have concentrated more on trying to rally support for 'those principles of life and policy from the lack of which we are suffering disastrous consequences'. But this, he concludes, would have been too demanding a task (and, he half-implies, a futile one).

The Criterion's missionary self-consciousness was such that one tends (as Eliot surely does above) to be rather more aware of what it 'stood for' in terms of ideology, than of what it actually achieved in terms of those 'repudiated' literary standards. There was no talented group of poets or novelists contributing to it regularly, and no sense of it encouraging particular literary movements. The championing of Eliot's own work and that of his contemporaries had been done, and done successfully, in other magazines before *The Criterion* began, and it is noteworthy that Eliot took no part in encouraging the resurgence of Imagism that occurred around 1930. The 'neo-Imagists' tended, of course, to be those

Americans like William Carlos Williams whom Eliot had 'betrayed' nearly twenty years before. When the *Imagist Anthology* appeared, it is significant that Eliot sent it to Harold Monro, a critic whose eye for the experimental he had special reason to remember. (Monro once turned down the chance to publish *Prufrock*.) Monro responded with fine Squirearchical contempt: 'for the rubbish of William Carlos Williams what excuse can be made by anybody? This kind of nonsense is enough to damn any book. The Twentieth Century has grown too old to include it any more in its magazines and anthologies. The joke has been made and the laughter has died away.'

One would be hard put to name any valuable *Criterion* discoveries. Good things appeared, of course: poems by William Empson and Hart Crane; Auden's *Paid on Both Sides*; Eliot's own *Waste Land* – and Eliot was particularly proud to have been the first English editor to publish Proust, Valéry, Cocteau and other Continental (mainly French) writers. During the 1930s he took up most of the good new poets and had many of them writing regular reviews. Geoffrey Grigson, George Barker, Charles Madge and Kenneth Allott were welcomed to the fold, along with Auden and Spender. They injected some needed rigour into literary-critical pages which had been dominated for too long by such figures as Humbert Wolfe and John Gould Fletcher. But none of these young writers could be described as Eliot discoveries, nor as especially close to the magazine's heart. They graduated to *The Criterion* by way of smaller and more adventurous periodicals. Most of what seem to have been Eliot's own protégés have since more or less disappeared from view. T. O. Beachcroft, for example, who wrote:

> Here no spring breaks,
> No warmth the barren stone unlocks;
> No herbs, grasses nor such green things break
> Through the iron rocks.

> Here no roots hold
> No fruits to bear,
> But year by year
> No season of living or dying can be told
> Here.

This is not an uncharacteristic contribution. One likely way of getting poems published in *The Criterion* was to lift lines out of *The Waste Land*. Like many original writers, Eliot had a deep weakness for pastiche of his own work.

In spite of its essential and, retrospectively, its debilitating faults, *The Criterion* enjoyed immense prestige, particularly during its early years, and mostly in literary quarters. The important thing about it, of course, was that it was edited by T. S. Eliot. Hart Crane wrote, on hearing that his 'Tunnel' section of *The Bridge* had been accepted: 'I have been especially gratified by the reception accorded me by *The Criterion*, whose director, T. S. Eliot, is representative of the most exacting literary standards of our times.' This must have been a fairly general view. Eliot was the leading poet of his generation; his approval had to be some kind of guarantee of excellence. The magazine's dubious ideology, the frequent turgidity of its set essays, the gradual drift away from literature into politics and then into the dense and dismal labyrinths of theology – none of this was likely to deter the admirer of Eliot's poetry from placing a high valuation on his practice as an editor. In 1930 Ezra Pound – who appeared in *The Criterion* surprisingly infrequently – was instructing the editor of *Hound and Horn* (a magazine which had set out to model itself on *The Criterion*):

> Don't sink into Criterionism. Criterion has printed in seven years about enough live stuff for one; if that... One cannot indulge continually in a diet of dead crow without its tainting the breath ... you cannot spend so much of your time analyzing the imperfections of dead and moribund writing without some odour of the undertaker's

establishment penetrating the pages of the review.

Pound had an excellent nose for such odours, but it was to be a few years before his view was unignorably justified by the actual contents of the magazine. In 1938, Julian Symons was probably speaking more than his own mind when he complained that the 'moral scale of values by which (*The Criterion*) judges literature and life is one that no longer has much meaning'.

It is ironical and appropriate that as *The Criterion*'s 'tendency' petered out into ludicrous irrelevance, the magazine began to show more vigour and purpose on the 'creative' side – the irony being, of course, that the writers who introduced this new vitality could hardly have been more hostile to the *Criterion* ideology. It is some kind of tribute to Eliot's open-mindedness in matters of purely literary criticism that he should have allowed this to happen in the dramatic way it did. But all the same, the last thing *The Criterion* will be remembered for is open-mindedness.

4

The Billhook

Although, looking back on his editorship of *New Verse*, Geoffrey Grigson has more than once regretted (or said he regretted) the magazine's vigorous use of what he has called the critical 'billhook', he himself in the intervening years has never quite abandoned his old weapon. Certainly he has not even begun to crumble into the bland, political equivocations that one has learned to expect from antique littérateurs. In many ways, Grigson's lively, jaundiced presence is as valuably unsettling as it ever was. He is a natural dissenter.

Even so, there is no disguising that he is a far gentler spirit now than when he was in command of what most people who remember it still think of as the toughest and most entertaining of all the little magazines. But then he could hardly fail to be. Few editors have trodden on so many important-looking toes with such uncomplicated relish as *New Verse* contrived to time and again throughout the 1930s. Nobody was entirely sacred; not even the magazine's own handful of hero figures. One by one the poets and poetasters of the day were handed their deserts – just or unjust. There was always more than enough vitriol to go round.

If there had been no more to *New Verse* than scandalous hostility to the pomposities and mediocrities of the age, Grigson would deserve our applause – perhaps even our gratitude. The magazine was never boringly malicious and the majority of its targets in fact did get what they deserved. But there was more. Above all, there was Auden. It was the presence of Auden and the glimmerings of a new wave in poetry which his presence seemed to be encouraging that provided the chief impulse behind the founding of *New Verse*. At the time of the magazine's conception, Grigson was in fact already an editor, toiling away on the book pages of *The Morning Post*. What he wanted from *New Verse* was perhaps an escape route from the ambivalence he felt in working for a Rightist paper; and indeed, he was to turn his *Morning Post* position into a positive advantage – *New Verse* was for a long time subsidized by the sale of the newspaper's superfluous review copies. He also wanted a place where he could publish his own poems ('if no one else would') and poems by the emerging young. And he wanted to clear the literary air – words like 'clean' and 'fresh' crop up time and again in his opening pronouncements.

This hygienic motive derived, one suspects, from *New Verse*'s other major influence – Wyndham Lewis. Grigson had run into Lewis not long after coming down from Oxford and had been pretty well bowled over by him (indeed remains so to this day). There is no doubt that much of *New Verse*'s pleasure in hatchet work can be traced directly to the Enemy's baleful, stimulating presence:

> He was wonderful to know, intellectually generous, more so than anyone I have met. I never understand the talk about Lewis as a monster; the Herbert Read talk; the Hemingway talk about the 'most evil' man he'd ever come across ... One grew up to think of Lewis as the hammer of the effete, in days of ridiculously correct Sunday journalism of the half-mind. And the *London Mercury*. And

Bloomsbury. And Edith Sitwell making a public monkey of herself in order to be celebrated. So Lewis seemed very sane, very serious, and modern; laying propositions down in front of you.

With disturbances like *Blast* and *The Enemy* behind him, Lewis was a marvellously correct presence to hover in the background of a new periodical in search of edge and vigour, and it is to his credit that – whatever his personal influence on Grigson (would *New Verse* have been quite so tough on Edith Sitwell without proddings from Lewis?) – he never attempted a Pound-style take-over. Nor did he make capital out of *New Verse*'s admiration. He was, as Grigson has acknowledged, a genuinely guiding spirit – one of the three to whom *New Verse* paid more or less unwavering homage:

> Under the great London shadows of Eliot and sardonic Lewis, and under those characters of the Empyrean who threw no shadow of a detectable presence, or a presence on which one could advance, a second or third newness was arriving. The planet Auden was up.

To hail this new planet; to give voice to Lewisian sardonics – these were the two obvious first incentives of the magazine.

New Verse No. 1 appeared in January 1933 and although it did offer the odd acerbity here and there (a description, for instance, of the current world of letters as 'a poisonous and steaming Gran Chaco of vulgarity, sciolism and literary racketeering'), the ruling tone was one of responsible solemnity. There was to be no 'complex or tiring manifesto', it was announced, and there was to be no political propagandizing. *New Verse* aimed to be a poetry magazine, no more, no less:

> Poets in this century and during this period of the victory of the masses, aristocratic and bourgeois as much as proletarian, which have captured the instruments of access to the public and use them to convey their own once timid and silent vulgarity, vulgarizing all the arts, are allowed

no longer periodical means of communicating their poems.

This haughtily Arnoldian note was not to last, but it is significant that *New Verse*, remembered now as the home of left-wing poets, should have opened with such determinedly apolitical assurances. The propagandists were lined up alongside other types of philistine and vulgarian as essentially the enemies of poetry – and therefore the enemies of *New Verse*. Thus there is in the first two numbers a marked insistence on the centrality of the magazine's strictly aesthetic concerns. 'Individuality is required,' Grigson wrote in No. 2. 'If there must be attitudes, a reasoned attitude of toryism is welcomed no less than a communist attitude.' And in No. 1, he declared that *New Verse*

> favours only its time, belonging to no literary or politico-literary cabal, cherishing bombs only for masqueraders and for the everlasting 'critical' rear-guard of nastiness, now represented so ably and variously by the *Best Poems of the Year*, the Book Society and all the gang of big shot reviewers.

It must have been difficult for the average reader of the day to immediately 'place' *New Verse*. It was pro-Auden, Spender and Upward and was prepared to concede that 'Day Lewis cannot make himself entirely a bad artist', but at the same time it was aggressively suspicious of any overt politics in poetry (Day Lewis, for instance, was accused from the outset of being 'too able to wither himself as a poet by being politically active') and suspicious too of the journalistic attentions that were beginning to get focused on Auden and his followers. A nice measure of the magazine's apparent oddity can be found in the attack on *New Country* that appeared in No. 2. Certainly the most severe lashing to be administered in any of the opening numbers, it denounces Michael Roberts for behaving in his preface 'as though he were G.O.C. a new Salvation Army or a cardinal presiding over a Propaganda'. Roberts's sin was one which *New Verse* frequently poured scorn on – any kind of band-wagoning enthusiasm for new trends was bound, in Grigson's view, to bury the genuine in a quagmire of pastiche: 'It disgusts me to find ... the good artist styed here with sentimentalists or ineffectual propagators.'

In the first five issues of *New Verse* this violent note is only rarely struck – the reviews, most of them by Grigson himself, are fairly rigorous (though in one of them Allen Tate is allowed to say of Stephen Spender 'his poetry is not surpassed by any other English poet since the war') but not really rancorous. Scorn, where it appears, is directed not at poets but at anthologists or critics, at those who treat poetry ill, whose attitude to the new is either negligent or opportunistic. In the fourth issue, *Scrutiny* is taken to task for its lack of interest in contemporary verse. Leavis's critical unreliability, we are told, is 'most obvious in his hard remarks on Mr Spender ... (he) cannot recognize creative generosity until years have passed':

> *Scrutiny*, if Dr Leavis wants some plain criticism, is too adolescent, too ready to accept the naiveties of ledger-criticism, informed with a little sour yeast of Eliot and Lawrence ... if *Scrutiny* is not to be the perfect bodybuilder for prigs it must change its formula.

The same resentment of academic indifference to what's currently being done appears in a review (in No. 5) of F. L. Lucas's pamphlet, *The Criticism of Poetry* – 'in his sciolistic pamphlet, bred of fear, presumption and petulance, the pathetic Mr Lucas denies merit to all contemporary criticism and poetry'.

The battle-lines were being drawn. On the one hand the Academy, on the other the bland idiocies of powerful entrepreneurs. And in between, the propagandists and politicizers. Against these, Grigson advanced the 'cleaner, fresher' poetry of – apart from Auden and Spender – new names like Gavin Ewart (his 'Phallus in Wonderland' in No. 3 necessitated a change of printers), Charles Madge, Norman Cameron, George Barker and – in No. 5 – David Gascoyne. The appearance of Gascoyne is of significance since it initiates *New Verse*'s brief and barely rewarding flirtation with Surrealism. This flirtation Grigson has recently acknowledged to have had more to do with an obedience to current fashion than with any real commitment, and certainly *New Verse*'s dealings with Surrealism look fairly half-hearted. But the fact that Grigson could be drawn into the thing at all (perhaps those surrealistic elements in early Auden seemed to provide an inviting endorsement of the movement) does suggest that after its energetic start, *New Verse* might well at this point have been suffering from that attack of indecision which so often afflicts little magazines once the first flush of enthusiasm has been gone through. In No. 6, Gascoyne was prominent, both with his own poems and with translations. Giacometti's 'Poem in Five Spaces' was accompanied by an article from Charles Madge on 'Surrealism for the English'. Madge's tone was guarded but respectful. He urges English poets to learn from Surrealism how to use 'the theory of metaphor and the double image'. Such usage, he predicts, will help further the 'development of his own tradition'. All the same, caution is also advised, and English bards are reminded that 'In France, the history of the poetic word has been very different from its history in England.' Whichever way one looks at it, the advice was acceptably meaningless; and sits oddly in a magazine which had already begun to pride itself on knowing exactly what it thought.

The Surrealist fad did not last long, and between numbers 7 and 11, one finds *New Verse* settling into what was to become its customary stride. The stress on criticism – of poets now rather more than of mere men of letters – becomes more evident, and the criticism itself more self-consciously belligerent. In No.7 *New Verse* takes the first of what were to be many bites from the hands that fed it. Randall Swingler and John Pudney were up for review: 'These writers have contributed a poem or two to *New Verse* but that would not excuse complimenting them kindly with lies or half lies ... Mr Swingler certainly, Mr Pudney perhaps, should give up poetry for politics or prose.' In the same issue, praise is lavishly bestowed on *One Way Song*, and there are poems by nearly all the now familiar *New Verse* names – Auden, Spender, MacNeice, Tate, Cameron. Poems aside, though, the issue is some kind of turning point – it is the edge of cruelty, of willingness to wound, that, however mildly, informs the Swingler review which signals the change. From this point on, the taste for blood develops into a positive appetite, and *New Verse*, which up to this point has had a handful of poets and a brave face, begins to cultivate a style. In No. 8 Ronald Bottrall is denounced as an imitator of Eliot (an oblique jibe, this, at *Scrutiny*) and in No. 9 another *New Verse* contributor is lovingly pinned to the mat. The victim this time is A. S. J. Tessimond. Note the access of sheer relish:

> Empty Room described p. 13, Sick Room described p. 29, Escalator and Tube Lift contrasted p. 31, Sea Port described p. 30, Wet City Night described p. 32, The Act of Meeting described p. 6, The Durable and Solid Expression of Architecture noted p. 18, Cat described pp 19, 20, Note of Music p. 24, Dance p. 28 and Nothing p. 25. Mr. Tessimond, you will see, is another simple poet.

By No. 12 Grigson had settled comfortably into his stride and this issue is – apart from the poems section – almost exclusively devoted to the joys of condemnation. The editor explains:

> It may have struck readers that several numbers have now gone by since a book either of poetry or criticism has been

praised in *New Verse*. This number contains more condemnation of books which I (and some others) hold to have been fingered much more delicately elsewhere than they deserve. Poetry now and poets are buttered by a number of very dangerous friends. Some friends, aunts or uncles, wish not to be left behind or forgotten; some like mice creep in through holes into this new-poetry mansion and warm their small noses at the fire and try to swell out to poet size (these always edit anthologies); some believe that poets should keep together, show a united front or backside, and never attack each other in the *Spectator*, the *Listener*, and other places where they and their friends write, no matter what banalities they may have committed. In this sense, *New Verse* must publish a decree absolute of divorce from any poet, new or bearded.

To prove he means it, Grigson goes on to swing blows at new books from both Day Lewis and (at long last) Stephen Spender. He follows this with a caustic examination of the contents of *The Year's Poetry* and then moves on to deliver the first of *New Verse*'s assaults on the family Sitwell, and on Edith in particular. Edith Sitwell was the ideal representative of all that Grigson most loathed in the literary world – she was society-literature, 'aesthetic, Firbankish and upper crust' – and once *New Verse* fastened its teeth in her, it never let her go. She became 'the old Jane', the 'scarecrow of an advanced fool farm', and so on. It is surprising that she had been allowed to go free for so long:

> And Miss Sitwell. In dealing with this lady and her brothers, silence has always been the rule in *New Verse*. 'The wisest way' I have held 'is not to name them but (as the Madman advised the Gentleman, who told him he wore a sword to kill his enemies) *to let them alone and they will die of themselves*.' Never before has the name Sitwell crept into *New Verse*. I doubt if it will ever creep in again.)

However this verse-writing vilifying lady has attacked myself, *New Verse*, and those who have written for it, with all her neurotic, feeble vigour, with inaccuracies, misquotations and abuse. The best comment on her book has been by Mr. Wyndham Lewis. He called it not a book but a dream; and a dream cannot well be attacked. Miss Sitwell's amazing misquotations, the amazing resemblances between parts of her book and parts of Mr Leavis's *New Bearings*, Mr Herbert Read's *Form in Modern Poetry* and my article on the *Cantos* of Ezra Pound have been exposed elsewhere, though incompletely and with too much kindness. It has given me some amusement to have my face slapped by this modern Della Cruscan but in the present condition of the 'literary world' satire, it has been proved, and reasoned reply cannot kill even the smallest micro-organisms of the pen, even the Sitwells; and I shall be content (since no doubt readers of *New Verse* long ago gave up esteeming their work) with saying just what I believe about these three versifying oddmedods: They have as writers a talent for perching head into wind, for appropriating, like bower birds, shining oddments of culture and for mimicking, like starlings, the products of more harmonious throats. Ignorance, deficiency in ideas and insensitivity they are able to defeat within themselves by tireless advertisement and by confiding in the ignorance, deficiency in ideas and insensitivity of reviewers, their gullibility and their day to day memory. They are everybody's highbrow artists, cartooning themselves for the mob as the 'queer men' of poetry. They have written nothing worth a wise man's attention for five minutes, but like the eels or 'obscure authors that wrap themselves in their *own Mud*' they are mighty pert and nimble. Eels live, though one skins them or cuts them into ten parts. Best leave these minimal creatures, these contemptible elvers, wriggling away in their dull habitat.

Later in the same issue, perhaps to prove that *New Verse* was showing no favouritism to the Sitwells, the attack on Spender was resumed and amplified by a reviewer who signs himself D.M.T. (Dylan Thomas?). Spender's *Vienna*, we are jauntily informed, 'leaves much to be desired; in the first place it leaves poetry to be desired'. Grigson's tone was nothing if not contagious and, warming to his task, the reviewer goes on to speculate on the reasons why 'the author of *The Rock*' should have chosen to publish a revolutionary propaganda-poem. The only sort of revolutionary Eliot would tolerate, it is concluded, would be one like Stephen Spender: 'the stand-in-the-corner, pat on the back young man who, by his insistence on the crudities of language and the tin thunder of naughty images, sets himself up immediately as the communist-intellectual type, pigeon-holed by *Punch*'.

If it was in fact Dylan Thomas who took Spender thus to task, he did not have to wait long for his own naughty images to come under examination. Thomas, along with George Barker, had received hospitality from *New Verse*, but neither had ever seemed to sit very comfortably in its clinical pages; they both seemed to have issued from that corner of now-forgotten, now – presumably – regretted interest in the Surrealists. The terms in which Thomas (in No. 13) came under fire might well have come in handy two years earlier. Attention is drawn to his 'monotony', his 'impurity of image', his 'awkwardness of syntax' – 'at times any word will do: caulk it in, if it's a nice word, and damn the meaning'. Uncharacteristically for a *New Verse* review that has settled into its splenetic stride, the piece ends with a faint whisper of advice and praise: 'He needs severity from himself; but he has more inside him and a more sceptical intelligence and writes more genuine prose (not to include poems) than most new poets.' Barker was not to enjoy any such spasm of editorial loyalty. A contributor to *New) Verse* almost from the start, he finds in No. 15 his latest book noticed under the heading 'Nertz'. Some of it reads as follows:

> Why has anyone published, does any one praise, does anyone read, the verse of Mr George Barker?
>
> Mr Barker's libidinal development has been upset. He is turned in on himself in a morbid narcissism, loving himself, and anxious to be loved, in order to preserve his own self-importance.
>
> I have never attempted, I am certain, to review more nauseating poems, and I have never read more inept juvenilia.

New Verse often seems to have rather strained itself to find fault with its own but here Grigson passes into something genuinely schizoid – as if the pleasure of raillery had somehow disconnected itself from its target. Or perhaps he had simply had a bad day at the office. Either way, George Barker might reasonably have considered himself somewhat maltreated, or complained that his poems were being used to feed an animus that was beginning to get out of control.

And the Barker review *is* usefully typical of the reverse side of all that is bracing and amusing in *New Verse*. And it is thus a useful measure of the magazine's achievement; set as it was on a course of mockery and destruction, *New Verse* managed astonishingly well to keep itself free of mere mud-slinging. Almost always, some genuine critical point was being made, some real weakness in the work at issue was being isolated. And more often than not the venom, when it appeared, was as much a rejoinder to the polite and tepid procedures of the general run of weekly book reviewers as it was to the specific book. This seems true of the following (and it is worth comparing the cheerful malice here with the murky savagery of the Barker piece). It's a review of *First Poems* by Rayner Heppenstall:

> We believe Mr R.H. as a poet to be absolutely a BORE.

He is a sluggish bore, a Hopkins-Binyon bore, a tangle of pimpled laurels bore*, a costive bore, a really I do not know Sir James Frazer bore; always absolutely a BORE. He is also a yearning, blind, deaf, word-gargling, 1930 book-bedded, prose-snipping, egg-bound bore, a bore not yet beyond B.O. breast-fingering poems, a bore pretending to purpose, a culture bore; this kind of King's Medal bore:

> These you are. Let be you chiefly that which slow
> Process of roots, with clutch on earth-stuffs that stir
> This thick plant-food into fire, signs, cannot blur,
> As pure response, pure act: which you will not know.

A BORE always as a poet, and a very small bore luckily.

* Since this bore declares, 'About half of these poems have appeared before: in *The Adelphi, Everyman, The Gryphon, The Listener, The New English Weekly, New Verse* ...' we declare that only one ever appeared in *New Verse* and we're sorry for that.

And so another egg is tossed from the nest. But it is unlikely that even Heppenstall believed that all this inventiveness was really being levelled at *him*. It clearly had much more to do with *New Verse*'s ambition to adopt a stance in relation to the whole world of contemporary letters – a stance that was unsolemn, uningratiating, incorruptible, that was courageous enough to make enemies and break friends. Although *New Verse* always kept one eye open for new poems, it often seemed to have more than two eyes open for new frauds.

By December 1935, when the Heppenstall review appeared, *New Verse* had settled into a fairly stable pattern. Each issue carried about a dozen poems (in addition to the established names a frequent contributor was Martin Boldero, one of Grigson's pseudonyms) and a clutch of about half a dozen book reviews. At odd times an 'Enquiry' would be attempted, with leading questions put to leading poets, and there had been special numbers on Hopkins and on Poets and the Theatre – both topics having evident relevance to the magazine's devotion to all things Audenesque. The Theatre number was in typical *New Verse* style, the anxiety to prove detachment from a vogue being a good deal fiercer than the interest in the actual subject. Both Auden and Spender had of course made their first steps in verse drama and the Group Theatre had begun to establish itself as the home of experimental left-wing plays. The theatre's title alone would have been enough to alienate *New Verse* and although the Theatre number gave space to Rupert Doone, the Group's leader, its real motive, one could hardly doubt, was to call the whole enterprise in question:

> The occasion for this number ... is the queer case in which poets in England now find themselves if they are interested in writing plays ... it is the Group Theatre which provides the queer case. The Group Theatre is not good enough – let us be frank – for the poets it is trying to train in dramatic sense. Its season this year and previous activities have been informed by the amateurism, it seems to outsiders, of pretending only to be serious, of pretending to have a group feeling and purpose (to the observer this 'groupishness' seems as false as an Oxford group) when it is socially-cum-aesthetically in the half-light and much less worldly than its chief poets; and technically in presentation and performance it has seemed as distressingly second-rate as the Old Vic, its actors knowing neither their own bodies, their own minds or the times they are living in.

This small outburst was, it transpired, in the nature of a warning shot. In the next issue (No. 19) Kenneth Allott, the magazine's assistant editor, followed up with (it *had* to happen) an attack on Auden and Isherwood's *Dog Beneath the Skin*:

> This is not a play so much as an imaginative Irish stew, a general store, a pot-pourri of variety acts of the simplified world which Mr Auden sees.

Bold words indeed from the disciples – and just for good measure this same heretical issue carried Grigson's now notorious 'stuffed goldfinch' review of Wallace Stevens ('an uneasy twinkle of sequins, describing thirteen ways of seeing a blackbird, forgetting the bird') and a marvellously terse appraisal of Hugh MacDiarmid's *Second Hymn to Lenin* – 'seventy-seven pages of unvarying twitter'.

The next four issues of *New Verse* trotted out fairly uneventfully – the only surprises having to do with phrase-making rather than with subject matter. Edmund Blunden was awarded his deathless title 'The Merton Fieldmouse', Michael ('The Mountaineer') Roberts was taken down from the shelf for another routine drubbing and Roy ('Mr Bullfighter') Campbell was repaid for his MacSpaunday jibes: 'Big swelling muscles holding up highly coloured bladders of bad air.' (It has been popularly supposed that Grigson was unfortunate enough to encounter those same swelling muscles at some literary gathering and lost his glasses in the ensuing skirmish.) It was not until No. 24 that a ripple of real novelty hit the magazine – the appearance of Mass Observation. Rather like *New Verse*'s dabblings in Surrealism, this new interest had a constant air of hopeful deliberateness about it. One can't, that is to say, believe that *this* leaden introduction to MO did not raise a few sardonic chuckles from the magazine's humorous editors:

> Mass Observation is a technique for obtaining objective statements about human behaviour. The primary *use* of these statements is to the other observers; an interchange of observations being the foundation of social consciousness. The statements are useful also to scientists who can each utilise them in his own way. The number of scientific interpretations of a given body of material is

only limited by the number of scientific interpreters. Poetically the statements are also useful. They produce a poetry which is not, as at present, restricted to a handful of esoteric performers. The immediate effect of MASS OBSERVATION is to devalue considerably the status of the 'poet'. It makes the term 'poet' apply, not to his performance, but to his profession, like 'footballer'.

It is hard to imagine the Grigson of a few years earlier giving space to these laborious philistinisms – although the limitations of his own critical stress on 'accuracy' had always been apparent (and never more so than in his sneer at Wallace Stevens). But there were no smiles either in this number or in the following one (No. 25) when the poetic consequences of the Mass Observation technique were horribly revealed in the shape of 'The Oxford Collective Poem'. Twelve undergraduates from Oxford were given the task of noting in a log 'the scene, event, subject, or phrase which had most occupied his mind during the day. The predominant image we preferred to be indicated by external rather than internal evidence.' The poem of eighteen lines that eventually emerged from the collected data was as follows:

THE POEM

Believe in the iron saints who stride the floods,
Lying in red and labouring for the dawn:
Steeples repeat their warnings; along the roads
Memorials stand, of children force has slain;
Expostulating with the winds they hear
Stone kings irresolute on a marble stair.

The tongues of torn boots flapping on the cobbles,
Their epitaphs, clack to the crawling hour.
The clock grows old inside the hollow tower;
It ticks and stops, and waits for me to tick,

And on the edges of the town redoubles
Thunder, announcing war's climacteric.

The hill has its death like us; the ravens gather;
Trees with their corpses lean towards the sky.
Christ's corn is mildewed and the wine gives out.
Smoke rises from the pipes whose smokers die.
And on our heads the crimes of our buried fathers
Burst in a hurricane and the rebels shout.

Presented with pride as comprehensively expressing 'the sense of decay and imminent doom which characterizes contemporary Oxford,' the Collective Poem could hardly have been more trundlingly mechanical and literary. The organizers clearly forgot that the undergraduate eye, far from seeing freshly, was bloodshot with reading. Someone must have pointed this out, though, for little more was to be heard in *New Verse* of the usefulness of Mass Observation; and thankfully readers were never exposed to the projected next experiment: 'the synchronous composition of a collective poem by bodies in different places and then a comparison of results.'

Also in No. 25 was to be found the definitive *New Verse* farewell to C. Day Lewis. Always a suspect figure, he was now roundly chastised for joining the selection committee of the Book Society: how, it was asked, did the poet reconcile this with his revolutionary memberships:

> The Book Society is a Limited Company pimping to the mass bourgeois mind and employing 'distinguished' members of the literary underworld, *adopters* of literature as a profession, writers each of no more real existence than a tick lost in the last five minutes of a cuckoo clock. On this Committee, Mr Day Lewis no doubt will be Change, Revolution, Youth, the Rising Generation. But this ends his stance as the poet writing thrillers (result: respectful, knowing reviews of each thriller) and establishes him as

the Thriller Writer, the Underworld Man, the yesterday's newspaper, the grease in the sink-pipe of letters, who has been posed for ten years as a spring water.

The assault ends with a contemptuous 'We can get along without him.' In fact, though, Day Lewis appeared in the very next issue – though the explanation no doubt was that this didn't count, since his appearance was merely to pay homage to the local deity. No. 26-27 was a double number on Auden: 'We salute in Auden (though we do not forget all that can be said against him) the first English poet for many years who is a poet all the way round.' Contributions ensued from Isherwood, MacNeice, Spender, Allott, Read, Edwin Muir and others – and, on the whole, none seemed able to remember anything that could be 'said against him'; the issue was an assembly of salaams, pure homage. But it was to be given a particular retrospective poignancy in No. 28. Auden had finally sinned, it was sorrowingly reported; he had accepted the King's Medal for Poetry. Grigson (who himself was beginning to look a bit vulnerable: had there not been an advertisement in the Auden number announcing his editorship of *The Year's Poetry*) did his best to get round it, and compared with the Day Lewis attack, his regrets are rather dismally muted. Even so, a sin's a sin:

> There are many possible explanations. We do not know the right one. If it is one of the hostile explanations which do Auden no credit – well, Balzac was not always as good as his poems. It may be true that the joke is much more on the medal than it is on Auden. Anyone who knows Auden will realize that, but there is no good reason for taking the Royal Medal, all the same. We rather regret that Mr Auden has taken it; we rather regret the office of Poet Laureate, and we rather regret that Mr Masefield ever had anything to do with establishing a Royal Medal.

A sad day indeed, and it is a sad fact that, from this point on, *New Verse* was never to be quite its waspish, absolutist, self.

Auden's 'compromise' had extorted a compromise from his disciples, and it must have been realized that one couldn't merely 'regret' Auden's misdemeanour whilst condemning Day Lewis as 'grease in the sink-pipe of letters' for his not incomparable folly. Whatever Auden did, *New Verse* couldn't get along without *him*.

There were to be five more numbers of *New Verse*, one of them a double number on *Commitment* (in which one detects an uneasiness in the attempt to reconcile the magazine's long stress on poetic individualism with its acceptance of the fact that – in 1938 – 'the aesthetic attitude is now decidedly out of place'). There were to be further, but somewhat enfeebled-looking onslaughts, and there were more poems. But the sting, the impetus had clearly begun to fade. In 1939 there was a single attempt to re-invigorate the magazine, with the hopeful issue of a New Series, but in May 1939 Grigson recognized that the time had come – and not just (or so it must have seemed) for poetry magazines. The final issue of *New Verse* appropriately carried a review by Grigson of Auden's *Twenty-Seven Sonnets*. It was correct that this most uncharitable of magazines should go out on a note of generosity – and of touching tribute to the talent which had inspired it from the start:

> *New Verse* came into existence because of Auden. It has published more poems by Auden than by anyone else; and there are many people who might quote of Auden: 'To you I owe the first development of my imagination; to you I owe the withdrawing of my mind from the low brutal part of my nature to the lofty, the pure and the perpetual.' Auden is now clear, absolutely clear of foolish journalists, Cambridge detractors and envious creepers and crawlers of party and Catholic reaction and the new crop of loony and eccentric small magazines in England and America. He is something good and creative in European life in a time of the very greatest evil.

5

Family Feuds

Some few years ago Norman Podhoretz revealed to a stunned world (in *Making It*) that if you wanted to get on in New York literary circles, there was only one way to go about it; you had to become a member of the Family. Podhoretz went on to name names, and to trace the tangled genealogy of this powerful body. And guess what? It all began not on some Sicilian mountainside but in the offices of the *Partisan Review*. And its Joe Colombos all had names like Rahv and Greenberg.

If the founding fathers of *Partisan Review* had in 1934 guessed for a second that what they were inaugurating would in twenty years or so be regarded as the smartest thing in town they would surely have choked on their orange juice and abandoned the whole project. Smartness was the last objective of those super-solemn young revolutionaries who belonged to the New York branch of the Communist-backed John Reed Club; what they were founding was a magazine of dire, momentous gravity, a magazine whose function was thoroughly explicit. Subtitled 'A Bi-Monthly of Revolutionary Literature,' the first *PR* appeared in February 1934, and its editorial (though no editor was named – simply a board with twelve members, Philip Rahv among them) left no room for any puzzlement:

> *Partisan Review* appears at a time when American literature is undergoing profound changes. The economic and political crisis of capitalism, the growth of the revolutionary movement the world over, and the successful building of Socialism in the Soviet Union have deeply affected American life, thought and art. They have had far-reaching effects not only upon the political activities of writers and artists but upon their writing and thinking as well. For the past four years the movement to create a revolutionary art, which for a decade was confined to a small group, has spread throughout the United States. A number of revolutionary magazines have sprung up which publish revolutionary fiction, poetry and criticism. Some of these are issued by the John Reed Clubs.
>
> *Partisan Review* is the organ of the John Reed Club of New York, which is the oldest and largest club in the country. As such it has a specific function to fulfil. It will publish the best creative work of its members as well as of non-members who share the literary aims of the John Reed Club.
>
> We propose to concentrate on creative and critical literature but we shall maintain a definite viewpoint – that of the revolutionary working class. Through our specific literary medium we shall participate in the struggle of the workers and sincere intellectuals against imperialist war, fascism, national and racial oppression, and for the abolition of the system which breeds these evils. The defence of the Soviet Union is one of our principal tasks.

A heavy read, indeed. And the history of *Partisan Review*'s first decade is really the history of how almost every one of these ponderously promulgated goals came to be not just abandoned but, in slow and painful stages, totally reversed.

The god didn't fail so much as grow horns and a tail.

In 1934, though, he was glowingly beneficent. The simple-minded enthusiasm for the idea of the Proletarian Writer was not by any means exclusive to *PR*, but *PR* was perhaps the one place where the reader could depend upon catching a glimpse of fine intelligences operating at their lowest level for the sake of what they conceived to be their highest principles. This spectacle alone gives the magazine's earliest issues a special kind of macabre fascination.

'We shall combat,' the first editorial concluded, 'not only the decadent culture of the exploiting classes but also the debilitating liberalism which at times seeps into our writers through the pressure of class-alien forces. Nor shall we forget to keep our own house in order. We shall resist every attempt to cripple our literature by narrow-minded, sectarian theories and practices.' In those opening numbers, *PR*'s house was not just in order; it was suffocatingly spick and span.

The first 'creative' contribution published in *Partisan Review* begins like this: 'During the time when Elmer Jackson and his crowd were making money out of the taxpayers of our country ...' Another story in the same issue starts: 'Many of the operators and pressers had worked for the Pretifit company for twenty years ...' Both yarns offer a devout and wholly uninspired naturalism with exemplary subject-matter the only obvious reason for their publication. And this was to become the stock ingredient of *PR*'s fiction department. Meanwhile, in the critical department, where the real business of the magazine went on, figures like James T. Farrell and Jack Conroy were being elevated to near-heroic status: a typical review would run as follows (this, by Granville Hicks, of Conroy's *The Disinherited*):

> ... a fine book, a very important addition to the growing body of American proletarian literature. There is no question why it is so good a book; it grows out of Conroy's own

experience as a worker. He has not only observed but has also participated in proletarian life, and he has a remarkable gift for portraying that life to the reader who is remote from it.

In other words, to almost any *Partisan* reviewer. There was nothing more praiseworthy than a literate who had actually done a day's *work* at some time in his life (a characteristic biographical sketch of new *PR* contributors would list any such credential with great pride), and in the absence of more than one or two such gems, the average review was obliged to pad itself out with rhetoric about the 'new spirit' or the coming dawn. In the second issue, Philip Rahv provides a perfect example of such spiralling self-persuasion:

> No hue and cry of propaganda, no lugubrious headshaking of wiseacres, and no amount of sneering on the part of those who persist in tracing their palsied hieroglyphics on the flypaper of bourgeois class impotence, can arrest its progress.

'It' being the proletarian novel. In the same issue, there appears a grovelling notice of *The Young Manhood of Studs Lonigan* and a savage onslaught against T. S. Eliot (Eliot is accused of 'rubbing shoulders with every myth and dogma which is used by capitalism to maintain itself. His gods are the caricatures and monsters of fascism'). The significant distinction between the two pieces is not one of preference but of tone; whereas the Farrell piece is effortfully pious, the Eliot attack is energetically indignant. And one could similarly contrast all the magazine's pro and con reviews in just this way. On the attack, it sounded almost human.

And, of course, men like Rahv were far too clever and cultivated not to see this for themselves. As early as the magazine's third issue (June-July 1934) there are in evidence the first tremblings of self-examination. A lengthy editorial by Rahv and Wallace Phelps (Phelps had been the author of the Eliot review) begins typically enough – 'The last year has seen a quickening in the growth of revolutionary literature in America' – but goes on to admit that there *are* contradictory trends within the proletarian literary movement. Many young writers, it was conceded, have declared themselves for Communism, have joined the John Reed Clubs and have all the right intentions, but have yet to arrive at 'a sufficient understanding of the meaning of such declarations in practice'.

> What does the present paucity of authentic revolutionary short stories prove? Most of our writers have not grasped the fact that workers' struggles cannot be written about on the basis of a tourist's visit.

A welcome insight – rendered somewhat more comforting, however, by its expansion by the editors into an attack on what they call 'fashionable leftism'. The objection to leftism was not that it produced bad writing, but that in its ingenuity it was able to project a 'smokescreen of verbal revolutionism'. It was non-authentic. At the same time, of course, authenticity itself was no guarantee of merit; merely a pre-condition. And worse still, it had to be confessed that merit in literature *did* have something to do with questions of 'perception' and 'sensibility' and – though Rahv and Phelps are not quite able to bring themselves to utter the dread word – Talent. Struggling beneath the burden of a programmatic revolutionism, an ancient critical banality could be discerned. *PR* was making progress.

The editorial closes with a grim and formal declaration of dissatisfaction:

> The editors of *Partisan Review* feel . . . that they have not yet succeeded in the tasks they have set for themselves. On the whole much of the published material has not measured up to our standards. We have not published as many experimental stories and poems as we would desire,

and neither has most of the criticism dealt with fundamental questions.

True enough. In the same issue we are offered a poem by Joseph Freeman which exhorts cigar-smokers to remember that Mexicans, Cubans, Uruguayans, Puerto Ricans 'sweat, ache, starve for the azure smoke-ring exciting tonight's new lay', a story by Edward Newhouse called 'Bum's Rush in Manhattan' which opens: 'When my rent was three days overdue the woman came into the room and said, Mister . . .' and carries on from there, and a review of Dos Passos which declares: 'I am not concerned here with discussing the qualities of Dos Passos' work as literature, but as revolutionary literature.'

The stress placed by Phelps and Rahv on the lack of experimentation in the work they had published was the first real sign that the *Partisan Review* writers had begun to consider how they might apply their critical theories to the recent achievements of the great modernist writers. In the very first issue, Eliot had been rapped, and Archibald MacLeish had been trodden underfoot; but in each case, it was their right-wing politics that provided the spur. There had also been scattered sneers at notions of 'pure art' or 'insulated art', but there had been no mention of specific modernist writers. In No. 4, though, Wallace Phelps writes a review of Malcolm Cowley's *Exile's Return* and uses it as an opportunity to muse upon this very problem. The piece can be seen as announcing the onset of what was to become over the years one of the magazine's more serious headaches:

> T. S. Eliot is one of the strongest influences on us. This is so probably because he is the only really important poet of the immediate past. And this is an impression which no writer, however revolutionary, can entirely escape . . . In his poetry, however reactionary its ultimate implications may be, Eliot has perfected a new idiom and tighter

rhythms for expressing many prevailing moods and perceptions. A proletarian Eliot would of course be an anomaly, but ...

No, it's not easy, and Phelps could hardly be said to have made a very elegant job of disguising his reluctance to credit Eliot with anything except those 'ultimate implications'; even so, the worry clearly is present and it represents one more step forward from the rally rhetoric with which Phelps feels obliged to close his review – his vision is, he says, of a 'thin line of maturing revolutionary writers who ... are clearing the road ahead for a great proletarian art'.

The immediate road ahead in fact produces first news from England of MacSpaunday. Day Lewis is praised for having achieved, with *The Magnetic Mountain*, 'perhaps the most important revolutionary poem as yet written by an Englishman' (elsewhere in the same issue is to be found his notorious 'why do we all, seeing a communist, feel small?'), and Auden is felt to have the makings of 'a master of political satire'. Spender fares less well – 'one cannot see in him', writes Alfred Hayes, 'the growth of a strong revolutionary lyric talent'. Things being what they were on the home front – even *PR* found it impossible to say much in favour of its own poets – the presence in England of something resembling a real movement was clearly more than welcome. And yet, in another sense, unwelcome. *Partisan Review* had now produced five issues and with each one the level of optimism had minimally sunk, and a report in this fifth issue of the national meeting of the John Reed Clubs makes it clear that it was soon likely to sink further. At the meeting, members of the 'writers' commission' had

> unanimously denounced the 'leftist' character of some aspects of our young revolutionary literature. They condemned those practices in our work that lead fellow-travellers to think that they must become revolutionary writers overnight. They directed a collective attack

against writing which consists of unconvincing, sloganized tracts disguised as poetry and fiction. Together they showed that a living revolutionary literature could grow only out of genuine aesthetic recreation of the class struggle.

Showed? We are not told how. But the balancing of the 'genuine aesthetic' against the 'sloganized tract', though abstract and still timorous, does signal the end of at least one stage of self-delusion. The kind of worries expressed in the Reed Club report were to be at the centre of the magazine for many issues to come, and were to be a key feature of the discussions which took place at a Writers' Congress organized by the Communist Party in May 1935 (and heavily reported in *PR*). But for all the tone of urgency with which the concept of a 'revolutionary literature' was confronted, in reviewers' asides, or in full-scale symposia (in issue No. 6 there is one such), there was always a residual timidity, a fear of pursuing certain key issues to the point at which contamination by bourgeois-aestheticism might possibly occur. Questions about the 'usable past', the admissibility of non-proletarian subject-matter, the indulgence of personal emotion; these keep cropping up but never quite get followed through. The formulation of the idea of 'leftism' had, of course, been immensely helpful in the sense that it provided an opportunity for attacking crucial aspects of the revolutionists' literary position without jeopardizing the position itself, but it also helped to generate an atmosphere of terror – the accuser ran the risk of accusation. Phelps and Rahv went further than anyone else had dared to in a joint article in *PR* No. 6; the piece amounts to a plea for an open-minded and respectful attitude to 'the literary heritage of America':

> There is no use whatsoever in talking about the usable past if we assume beforehand that nothing is usable save that which is near-Marxian. Tradition supplies us with a basis

FAMILY FEUDS 107

for formal criteria, with a source of artistic training and with currents of influence.

Dangerous talk, and the authors were promptly rebuked by Granville Hicks for being too 'lofty' and for a bourgeois-style scornfulness about their fellow Marxists. But the point did get made, and if one sets the Rahv-Phelps piece alongside Edwin Rolfe's article on American poetry in the same issue, one sees just how far at least two of *PR*'s editors (Rolfe was also on the magazine's board) had allowed themselves to travel. Rolfe is still firmly stuck at the banner-waving stage:

> Only the revolutionary poets can today claim possession of the qualities which nurture and feed a great art. Only the poets who announce change, who as men are certain of the road they travel, can herald a new day in American poetry.

Rolfe proceeds from here to write off practically the whole of the American poetic heritage and in precisely the crude terms which Rahv and Phelps had been objecting to. Sooner or later, it must have been clear to all concerned with the revolutionary goal, the arguments would have to come out into the open, enmities would have to be declared, and hypocrisies either confirmed or abandoned.

In its eighth number *Partisan Review* issued the following cryptic announcement:

> Beginning with this issue *Partisan Review* will not be published as the organ of the John Reed Club of New York but as a revolutionary literary magazine edited by a group of young Communist writers, whose purpose will be to print the best revolutionary literature and Marxist criticism in this country and abroad.

The 1935 Writers Congress' was in fact the occasion for

this turning point – the Congress had decided to disband the John Reed Clubs and to replace them with a more integrated League of American Writers. This decision meant the death of several Reed Club publications, but for the *Partisan* it meant a major step towards true independence. There was talk of turning *PR* into the new League's official magazine, but this came to nothing. Which is just as well, for three months after the 1935 Congress, the communists threw both their friends and enemies into disarray with the announcement of the Popular Front. Looking back, many of the Congress's fervent delegates must have felt duped; at any rate, the founding of the League struck many as having been merely a preparation for the Party's hospitable new policies.

For a year after the Congress, *Partisan* clearly hadn't made up its mind how it intended to use its independence from the Party, nor indeed had it decided how much independence it really wanted. During 1936 it entered into a merger with another Marxist magazine, *The Anvil*, and even retitled itself *Partisan Review and Anvil*. It was not a particularly fruitful collaboration, and the five monthly issues that came out under this title had a distinct air of marking time – the early optimism was quite dead, suspicion of the Soviet Union was deepening, but not to the point where any decisive new direction could be confidently followed. In October 1936 the magazine suspended publication altogether, and the whole of the next year was spent in silent self-appraisal. Silent, at any rate, as far as the magazine was concerned; in fact, both Rahv and co-editor William Phillips wrote book reviews in other papers, and with each review they wrote, to move more and more into an openly hostile attitude to the new Party line – a line which, in literary terms, involved the abandonment of the old revolutionary intensities in favour of a willingness to court anti-fascist support from the liberals. In non-literary terms, it meant turning a blind eye to the Moscow Trials, regarding Roosevelt as a friend, Trotsky as a traitor, and so on. The whole thing was, as much as anything else, an insult to the intelligence, and both Rahv and Phillips had been keeping the intelligence on too tight a rein for far too long.

So too, in different ways, had the two new figures who during this year drifted into the *Partisan Review* orbit – two Yale chums who had co-edited a college literary magazine and thence moved into utterly distinct areas of frustration: Dwight MacDonald to write for the Luce magazine, *Fortune*, and F. W. Dupee to become, albeit briefly, literary editor of *New Masses*. Though without Rahv's backlog of almost entirely wasted effort in the Party cause, they shared his contempt for the cause's hypocritical new look, and they shared too his developing interest in Trotsky – the supreme figure of the outlawed intelligence. MacDonald and Dupee had one other vital asset, as far as the magazine was concerned; they were in touch with another friend from Yale – the painter George L. K. Morris, and Morris was prepared to finance an independent publication of the kind that *PR*, if resurrected, would surely have to be. Since the dissolution of the Reed Clubs, Rahv and Phillips had had to keep the magazine going out of their own resources and with help from friends, and financial trouble had played some part in the decision to suspend *PR*. By the end of 1937 *Partisan* was reconstructed, both financially and intellectually, and in December of that year the first issue was ready to appear (its rumoured preparation had been the subject of continued taunts and sneers from the Party press). The new editorial board comprised Rahv, Phillips, MacDonald, Dupee, Morris and (reputedly brought in as a result of pro-Trotsky remarks overheard at a cocktail party) Mary McCarthy. And the editorial lived up to all the ugly rumours: the new *Partisan Review*, it declared,

> is aware of its responsibility to the revolutionary movement in general, but we disdain obligation to any of its

organized political expressions. Indeed we think that the cause of revolutionary literature is best served by a policy of no commitments to any political party. Thus our underscoring of the factor of independence is based, not primarily on our differences with any one group, but on the conviction that literature in our period should be free of all factional dependence.

Disclaimers registered, the writer (Dupee) then went on to attend to those 'differences with any one group'. Allegiance to the Communist Party, he asserted, induces in writers an automatic political response which must in turn induce an artistic irresponsibility:

> And the Party literary critics, equipped with the zeal of vigilantes, begin to consolidate into aggressive political-literary amalgams as many tendencies as possible and to outlaw all dissenting opinion.

Thoroughly outlawed by this stage, the dissenting voice grows firmer and more savage:

> Formerly associated with the Communist Party, *Partisan Review* strove from the first against its drive to equate the interests of literature with those of factional politics. Our reappearance on an independent basis signifies our conviction that the totalitarian trend is inherent in that movement and that it can no longer be combatted from within.

The 'old movement' will, it is predicted, turn now for reinforcement to academicians, to 'yesterday's celebrities and today's philistines', and with each new political tragedy its official critics will call the louder for a literature of good cheer. *Partisan*'s 'new grouping', it is further prophesied, will come under repeated attack by Party hacks and could expect to be branded as either Trotskyist or fascist – or, on a really good day, as both:

> Every effort, in short, will be made to *excommunicate* the

new generation, so that their writing and their politics may be regarded as making up a kind of diabolic totality; which would render unnecessary any sort of rational discussion of the merits of either.

PR vowed to stand firm against hostilities of this nature, but also vowed not to fall into the same trap itself – in other words, the magazine would take care not to allow any writer's known connection with the Party to influence the way his work was criticized. *Partisan Review* was to be first and foremost a cultural magazine and would be open to any tendency which is 'relevant to the literature of our time'.

Marxism in culture, we think, is first of all an instrument of analysis and evaluation; and if, in the last instance, it prevails over other disciplines, it does so through the medium of democratic controversy. Such is the medium that *Partisan Review* will want to provide in its pages.

One can detect the soft pedal in these closing promises – the asserted 'open-ness', the lack of animosity towards Party writers, the wish for 'democratic controversy'. The lack of any firm stress on the 'revolutionary' literary goals which the magazine's editors all in fact shared can be viewed as an effort, albeit tactical, to come half way to meet the Party's depoliticizing of critical discussion and thus ensure that jibes about Trotskyism would be made just that bit more difficult. Although *Partisan*'s position in relation to the Communists was now entirely clear, it would not have been in their interests at this stage to have seemed too wild-eyed in their revolutionary commitment. Indeed, the total impression given by this first leader is of an effort for sweet reason – *they* were not going to play their opponents' dirty game.

The contents of the new *PR* were impressive enough for the editors to afford a little coolness – set beside earlier numbers, it is like a different magazine; genuinely more open, overwhelmingly more subtle and sophisticated in its critical approach, and offering a number of undeniably very promising new names. It's worth simply listing: a story by Delmore Schwartz, a poem ('The Dwarf') by Wallace Stevens, Edmund Wilson on Flaubert, Lionel Abel on Silone, an anti-Franco prose poem (with four etchings) by Picasso, poems by James Agee, an extract from a new novel by James T. Farrell, and an analysis by Dwight MacDonald of the *New Yorker*'s social attitudes. There is barely a weak moment in the whole issue – certainly, the first issue of the *Partisan Review* that can be read today with pure pleasure and not just out of curiosity. At the back of the magazine there was evidence, in a new section called *Ripostes,* that all was not in fact going to be calm and creative. Quoting headlines from the Party press about the new *PR* (e.g. 'A Literary Snake Sheds its Skin for Trotsky', *Daily Worker*), the author takes a few elegant and icy swipes at the 'simple-minded fanaticism' of the opposition. The first well-aimed shot in a battle that was going to occupy rather more of the magazine's space in future issues than, say, the poems of Wallace Stevens – or of anyone.

> But we shall not turn our face from you, O glorious and grieving Russia. If first you were an example to us, now, alas! you show in what engulfing sands a revolution can sink.

This, from an anti-Soviet diatribe by André Gide, was the appropriate star item in the second issue of the reconstructed *Partisan Review*. Although good poems and stories continued to be given space, and although a lot of the criticism – especially by Edmund Wilson and by Rahv himself – continued to be fine, and not noticeably fettered, the magazine's real energy during the next few years was to be political; specifically, anti-Stalinist. There was, of course, a literary motive behind the politics of *PR*; that is to say, the politics were always those of literary men, of men who wished to preserve the truth-seeking functions of literature against the philistinism and opportunism which they abhorred in the politics (and thus the literature) of their opponents. But these were not years in which literature could be defended merely by saying that it should be, and the distinction of *Partisan* – whatever one thinks of the position (or, as things turned out, positions) of the *Partisan Review* – was that it went into its political debate with an expertise and a practicality which one doesn't expect from literary men. They might have been wrong a lot of the time, but they were not starry-eyed.

A piece by Philip Rahv in the issue (Vol. 4 No. 3) of February 1938 is a striking instance of the advance in sheer political common-sense that the magazine had achieved since it started out. Its subject is in fact crucial to precisely this advance: a comparison between the Writers' Congress of 1935 and the Writers' Congress of 1937, a comparison which, for Rahv and for the *Partisan*, amounts really to a study of How We Grew Up:

> Today revolutionary thinking in literature has virtually come to an end – at least so far as concerns those who once wrote and talked most about it. To consider the background of the two congresses, the amazing contrast between the first and the second, and the political mystifications employed by the party that staged them, will help us to understand how this has come about.

Rahv then goes on to itemize the subtle and not so subtle shifts of attitude and terminology that had taken place since (and he puts insufficient stress on *this* point) *PR* glowingly welcomed and attended the first Congress: what used to be 'workers' were now 'the people', what used to be 'the struggle against *imperialist* war and fascism' was now simply against 'fascism', what used to be an '*international* class struggle' was now 'Spain' (and there the class struggle was a simple one: between fascism and 'democracy'), what used to be a capitalist system 'rapidly crumbling before our eyes' was now simply not referred to – 'Here in the United States all we had to do (1937-style) was to encourage trade unionism and defend what we already possess.' And as for revolutionary writing – by 1937 the Congress had transmuted that once burning concept into just another dirty word.

Rahv is savage and witty about those who had between the two Congresses shown themselves capable of performing the required about-turns and the whole piece, though suffused with anger and disappointment and contempt, is never finally intemperate – as much as anything else, and not unexpectedly, it is a first-rate piece of literary criticism, a pioneer study of the art of double-think. And there is no sign of the soft-pedal in Rahv's categorical conclusion:

> To expect a bureaucratic authoritarian regime to nourish a truly critical, revolutionary consciousness in art is to expect miracles. Already the Stalinists have introduced into their literary organs the methods of calumny and frame-up. It is impossible for the intellectual to make the moral and political compromises that Stalinism demands of him without betraying himself.

The preoccupation with the domestic hypocrisies involved in the Stalinist position continues through most of 1938 to be central to *Partisan*, rather suffocatingly so. Herbert Solow contributes an intricate account of the gymnastics performed by *New Masses*, listing those erstwhile Enemies of Mankind who had been magically turned into Pillars of the Congress, and indeed barely an issue goes by without *New Masses* coming in for a gloating rebuke of just this kind. The trouble is that there is so *much* evidence that the trial hardly seems worth spinning out.

What does not appear in these issues is any development of *PR*'s own self-described position as a journal of so-called revolutionary literature. There can be no question but that the Stalinists' new soft-line policy towards liberal writers made it difficult for *Partisan* to be as open in its critical explorations as it might have been – not wishing to seem hard-line itself, it did not wish either to seem soggily hospitable. The Party, by simply disposing of the concept of a revolutionary literature, had also disposed of that simplistic critical position which in 1935 was beginning to provoke dispute. Ironically enough, had the Party not got there first, *Partisan* itself would by 1937 have been arguing for a more open-minded approach to non-revolutionary writing – albeit for entirely different, and immeasurably more noble, reasons. As it is, the problem effectively gets shelved, and the magazine fluctuates between on the one hand the reiteration of revolutionist literary concepts and on the other the non-application of these concepts; they don't seem to affect what gets printed, or praised. Thus it is possible for Dwight MacDonald to write of the death of Eugene Jolas's *Transition* that it

> is symptomatic at once of the decay of bourgeois culture, even in its most 'advanced' strata, and of the impossibility of maintaining an above-the-battle attitude in a period of great social tension

and yet for *Partisan* to keep its doors open to the kind of modernist, or advanced-bourgeois, writing which *Transition* had been fostering.

But then events in Europe were moving fast, and horribly, enough by this time for MacDonald's 'above-the-battle' sneer to seem less philistine than it is. And *Partisan* itself was beginning to realize that there was something a bit above or indeed to one side of the battle in its own obsession with the goings-on of New York Stalinists. With the Fall 1938 issue (almost double the usual size and announced as the first quarterly issue of the magazine) there is a distinct broadening of the magazine's range of concerns. As the 'fascist threat' in Europe became more and more unignorable (*PR* had tended to play it down rather than play into the hands of Stalinists) a new internationalism begins to infiltrate the anti-Soviet obsession, and it is with enthusiasm that *Partisan*'s editors give their endorsement to André Breton's proposal for an International Federation of Revolutionary Art. The attraction of Breton's plea was that it permitted, in the name of literature, hostility to both Stalinism and fascism:

> In both Germany and (if reports may be believed) in the Soviet Union, artists have been reduced to the status of domestic servants, whose task it is to glorify it on order, according to the worst possible esthetic conventions.

The only defence was for artists of the left (and did not Trotsky say that all artists must by definition now be of the left?) to seek a common ground: 'Marxists can march here hand in hand with anarchists' – indeed, others can join in too provided that they 'uncompromisingly reject the reactionary police-patrol spirit represented by Joseph Stalin and by his henchman, Garcia Oliver'. Hitler seems to have been overlooked by this stage in the argument – but no doubt they meant to put him in.

If *Partisan*'s anti-Stalinism was by now enlarging itself into anti-totalitarianism, it was also narrowing into an aggressive pacifism – war would not stop totalitarianism, it would simply spread it. In the Spring issue of 1939 Dwight MacDonald spelt out the magazine's position:

> If there is one point that needs no laboring, it is that a modern war cannot be fought without universal conscription, without outlawing strikes and shackling the unions, without suppressing all dissenting opinion and handing the national economy over to the ruling class ... The final result of a war against foreign fascism will be the introduction of domestic dictatorship.

The point might have seemed to need no labouring, but it was to be laboured time and again throughout the next two years, and to be clung to with increasing desperation. From the outbreak of the European war, *Partisan*'s content was to become more and more heavily political – there was to be the odd poem or short story, and the occasional critical 'study', but by and large War was the issue, and *PR* knew exactly where it stood. Demolishing pro-war positions became as engrossing a task as exposing Stalinist hypocrisies had been – and with the announcement of the Hitler-Stalin pact, *PR*'s polemical contentment could hardly have been more complete. The pact really was too bad to be true, and one could not expect the magazine to succeed in eliminating altogether a note of triumph from its condemnation. With the issue of Fall 1939 – the first to be published since the outbreak of war, *PR* wrote as follows:

> So far the most important result of the war has been the exposure of the real political content of Stalinism. Ever since Hitler came into power, the Third International has posed as the great champion of the democratic masses against the menace of fascism. But with the first gun fired against Poland, its big pretensions fell away, its humanitarian vapourings condensed into cynical realpolitik...
> Stalin has been transformed overnight from an international philanthropist, whose pipe was an index of his philosophical benevolence, into a Metternichian power politican, his pipe-puffing now signifying preternatural guile.

Some slight move forward from the-war-equals totalitarianism position was clearly required by this new event, and in analyzing Stalin's motives *Partisan* contends that 'realizing the insecurity of his régime, Stalin, like Chamberlain who also fears revolution above all things, has one basic objective: to avoid war at all costs'. The obvious deduction to be drawn from this view, that war creates revolutionary situations, is not in fact pursued. The problem is that *Partisan* is against war at all costs, and so too – it now transpires – is Stalin; the only acceptable explanation can be that Stalin's avoidance of war is just another extension of his totalitarian designs. But then ... totalitarianism used to thrive on wars. A difficult one, and *PR*'s analysis can best be described as hasty. The editorial scurries off into rhetoric at the earliest opportunity, with a vision of 'the masses in each nation fighting not against their brothers across the border but against their own capitalist governments'. Some such vaguely evoked effort of international revolution is, we are assured, 'the only force that can either bring into being real democracy or make war and fascism unnecessary. This is the alternative which our liberals find either too Utopian or too bloodthirsty.' Or maybe even both.

In the first issue of 1940 there is still a certain amount of crowing over the discomfiture of the *New Masses* brigade, and James T. Farrell pretty well rounds off the triumph by answering a suggestion by John Chamberlain in the *New Republic* that Stalinists disillusioned by the Pact should form a united front with those who were disillusioned long before the Pact was signed. Farrell's reply to this is admirably terse: 'When I go to a dentist to have a tooth extracted and my jaw is broken in the process, I will not return to have more work done by the same man.'

Rather more important kinds of discomfiture were of course being experienced in Europe, and in the same issue there is an article by Philip Rahv which is anything but flushed with triumph. Titled 'What is Living and Dead in Marxism', it in fact represents an important, almost fatal, turning point for *Partisan Review*. Rahv acknowledges that to ask of Marxism that most basic of all questions is to take his ideological life into his hands, and he approaches it with proper trepidation. Why is it, he asks, that since 1917 'the failure of the socialist cause has been continuous and disastrous'; why is it that the proletariat has allowed this to be so?

To ask basic questions of Marxism was bad enough, but to ask them of the sacred proletariat was near to suicidal. None the less, Rahv asks away. He cites Trotsky's explanation that the fault has not been that of the proletariat but of those false leaders who have duped them, but refuses to accept it. Why do they let themselves be duped, he wants to know – and duped so often, and on such a grand scale:

> We detect in Trotsky's formulation a kind of backhanded admission that the working class is intrinsically lacking in sufficient independence and political self-definition to check and control its leadership.

If this is so, then why not, Rahv asks, admit it? Getting bolder with every sentence he goes on to deliver the killer punch:

> It is time for Marxists to be rid of the absurd convention, essentially moralistic and in part a carry over from Christian sentimentality about the 'meek and lowly', that plain speaking about the proletariat is somehow indecorous, if not actually impermissible.

Having gone so far, Rahv hesitates to go further. The problem is a problem and ought to be discussed, he says, but he does not pretend to be able to offer a solution, and nor would he wish to be thought to have set out 'to deny revolutionary status to the working class'. Then, as if realizing that he *has* hesitated, he *does* go further. There are other Marxian sacred cows that ought to be examined: for instance, all that 'history is on our side' mysticism, and 'the fetishism of economy' which it encourages. Here too

> is diseased tissue which it is not enough merely to cut away. The job of replacing it must be approached creatively, not as a means of appeasing the timorous and derelict.

The article ends with a small flurry of forestalling sneers at the motives of other 'revaluers'; there is a difference, Rahv explains, between 'panicky fugitives' and 'daring explorers'.

Rahv had given earlier hints that he had become disenchanted with most of the old rhetoric about 'revolutionary writing' and had been shifting his critical position more and more towards some kind of cultural elitism by attempting to endow the 'intelligentsia' (those few who defended the old and created the genuinely new forms of culture which totalitarianism was committed to destroy) with some kind of revolutionary status, but this article was his first explicitly political recantation. It could not have been more significant that it appeared in the same issue as Eliot's *East Coker* (an editorial *coup* which was to bring a number of complaining letters from *PR*'s readers: letters which, interestingly enough, were met with the reply that 'It is coming to be something of a revolutionary act simply to print serious creative writing') – the old split between the magazine's literary *avant-gardeism* and its political ideals was by now barely disguised, and Rahv's steady progress away from hard-line Marxism was to involve another split – between the members of *PR*'s editorial board.

In the issue of March–April 1941 Dwight MacDonald and Clement Greenberg published a joint statement called '10 Propositions on the War' – a fairly straightforward reiteration of the magazine's original anti-war position, framed on this occasion as a critique of the so-called 'lesser-evil' policy, which had recently been outlined in the magazine by Stephen Spender. 'The alternatives the lesser-evil policy of supporting Roosevelt-Churchill presents are: military defeat, owing to the superiority of fascism in total warfare, or victory under a fascist system of our own.' What MacDonald and Greenberg were doing, in effect, was bringing into the open arguments that had been simmering internally for months. Rahv had been allowed to use the editorial 'we' in his article; MacDonald and Greenberg were simply making it clear that no such 'we' existed any longer. In the issue of November-December 1941 Rahv took up the challenge, and attacked the MacDonald-Greenberg piece for its 'academic revolutionism'. He accused its authors of living in the past, of refusing to 'see anything which does'nt fit into their apocalyptic vision of a single cleansing and overpowering event which will once and for all clear away the existing social system'. Rahv went on to say his last goodbyes to the anti-war position – the defeat of Hitler in Europe was the 'pre-condition' of any progressive action in the future.

As Greenberg and MacDonald point out in their reply to Rahv, he adopts a pro-war position on behalf of Europeans, but falters at the last fence by declaring that the war 'is not yet our war' (ie America's):

> What exactly is our co-editor's position? It is a position for which he refuses to take any moral or intellectual responsibility. He knows only too well upon what he is relying to protect us from Hitler. He realizes the emptiness, the shabby hypocrisy of the present British and American war aims. Like Macbeth, he would like to profit by the crime without committing it.

Strong stuff, and the editors were right in deciding that readers ought to be told all over again just what *Partisan Review* now stood for. In the first issue of 1942 a formal statement was published:

> For some time, as recent issues of the magazine have made clear, the editors have disagreed on major political questions. The complexity of the world situation, indeed, is reflected in the fact that no two editors hold the same position on all major issues. The actual outbreak of hostilities has not altered this line-up. It is clear, therefore, that *Partisan Review* can have no editorial line on the war. Its editors will continue to express themselves on this issue as individuals.

With Pearl Harbor, Rahv had come to decide that the war really was, after all, 'our war', but MacDonald had stood firm. And the divergence of opinion between these two key figures was not to be healed in the pages of *Partisan Review*. The uneasy agreement to continue the magazine without any 'editorial line' could hardly last, but it did in fact last longer than might have seemed possible at the time. But to achieve this, *PR* was obliged to sacrifice much of its edge, its self-assurance. The issues were muddied throughout 1942 by two controversies – both of them central to *Partisan*'s own internal disagreements but neither sufficiently domestic to exacerbate the split. George Orwell's 'Letters from England', which were both anti-pacifist and pro-revolutionary (the war had to be fought to stop Hitler but could have the advantage for socialists of creating revolutionary situations in Britain) provoked a spirited argument among English contributors, an argument that usefully mirrored the disagreement between Rahv and MacDonald. And an article by Sidney Hook attacking the new wave of religiose anti-intellectualism that had resulted, in his view, from the 'failure of nerve' among disappointed thirties radicals also set off a continuing debate that helped to keep tempers in check. There was, too, the residual advantage of Rahv and MacDonald having separate but, in this instance, complementary cultural interests: Rahv's orthodox literary-critical concerns balanced by MacDonald's preoccupation with the emerging 'popular arts'.

But all these factors merely papered over the cracks, and MacDonald's frustration was not helped by the fear that if he really did let rip with the anti-war argument, the magazine might simply be closed down by the government. He would have been prepared to take that chance on his own and indeed during the summer of 1943, when the magazine ran into a financial crisis, he almost did assume control. When this didn't come off his choice was to remain, virtually gagged and completely isolated (Greenberg had left in 1943 to join, of all things, the Air Force), or to leave. He left, and his letter of resignation, with Rahv's and Phillips's reply, appeared in the last issue of that year:

> Dear Colleagues:
> Please accept my resignation from *Partisan Review*, effective next issue. I regret severing connections with a magazine to which I have given much time and effort. I feel however that the divergence between my conception of the magazine and your own has become too great to be bridged any longer. This divergence is partly cultural: I feel *Partisan Review* has become rather academic, and favor a more informal, disrespectable and chance-taking magazine, with a broader and less exclusively 'literary' approach. But the divergence is mainly political.
> When we revived *Partisan Review* in 1937, it was as a Marxian socialist cultural magazine. This was what distinguished it from other literary organs like *Southern Review* and *Kenyon Review* and this orientation, in my opinion, was responsible for much of the magazine's intellectual success. The war, however, has generated sharp political disagreements. Not only has the Marxist position been reduced to a minority of one – myself – but since Pearl Harbor there has been a tendency on the part of some editors to eliminate political discussion entirely.

MacDonald went on to predict that from now on *Partisan Review* would become a merely cultural journal and that the thorny field of politics would be left to people like himself: his intention therefore was to start his own new publication in the autumn (he did, and it was called, quite baldly, *Politics*).

In their reply the remaining editors accuse MacDonald of having been 'carried away by his political passions'; he had wished to turn *PR* into a political magazine with literary trimmings. They also accuse him of subordinating literary judgement to political ideology – and that their disagreement with him was not at all dissimilar to that which had led to *PR* breaking with the Stalinists five years before.

What is significant in this reply is that, although the editors reject, almost parenthetically, MacDonald's description of himself as the only Marxist on the board, they go to no great lengths to assert that *Partisan Review* is still a magazine with any clear political direction, let alone any political passions. The almost touching thing about the exchange is that each party is completely right about the other. For *Partisan* to have survived in any even quasi-revolutionist posture it would have had to go entirely MacDonald's way; for it to have survived as a magazine of literature (which it could hardly be said to have been, except intermittently, for quite a time) it would have had to strip itself of the last vestiges of its original embattlement. It did the latter, and looking back over *Partisan Review*'s first decade – the agonizings, the shifts and the revisions, the wrong prophesies and the hedged issues – one has to wonder how it took so long. It might be contended that only men of principle could have gone through such contortions so, of course, could fools. *Partisan*'s great strength throughout was that it was never as foolish as its principles sometimes made it look.

6

Styles of Despair

Suppose a remarkable urchin turned out the dirty lining of his magic pocket, in which he had casually collected the pubic hairs of a lion, two inches out of an indecent masterpiece by Fuseli, some recollections from Webster, a couple of Pleiades, and a comet, two or three stumps of coloured chalk, a tooth, some screwed-up counterfoils from sixpenny postal orders, nail-parings, a sucked-out tin of condensed milk, a pill-box of maggots, and one or two of Joanna Southcott's chests. Suppose this pile were to be divided into *mergbild* poems and short stories – there would be *The Map of Love*.

In 1940, there would have been no prizes for identifying the author of this piece of jolly waspery. Readers of *New Verse* had come to take for granted both the tone and the procedure. And with *New Verse* dead, they were no doubt delighted to find at least its editor surviving into the opening number of *Horizon*, a new monthly 'review of literature and art'. Small magazines were folding up on all sides as editors and contributors began to be scattered by the war, and the London literary scene was either fragmenting altogether or retreating into nervous depression. There were more important things to think about than new poems. And besides, look what had happened to the best of the new poets – Auden was safely in the States. It was therefore brave but odd of Cyril Connolly (and his assistant Stephen Spender, from whose flat the first issues of *Horizon* were put out) to attempt to maintain some continuity, some belief that the arts were still worth worrying about, or working for. But what continuity, many readers must have asked, could genuinely be hoped for at a time like this? Certainly, Grigson's admirers were to be disappointed; his first poetry review in the new venture was to be his last and it was soon clear that *Horizon* was to be very different from *New Verse*.

Astringency, polemical verve, creative certainty; none of these qualities was to distinguish Cyril Connolly's editorial career. Where *New Verse* had been in on the beginnings of a new literary wave, *Horizon* was in on the end of it. The thirties movement was over, and one of *Horizon*'s first tasks was to give it a decent burial – and to do so without any idea of what was coming next, of what the 'forties movement', if there was to be one, might possibly be like.

Right from the first issue (which appeared in January 1940) this puzzlement was made explicit: *Horizon*'s readers were warned not to expect too much from any magazine that attempted to give true voice to the current climate. Everything was too confused:

> The moment we live in is archaistic, conservative and irresponsible, for the war is separating culture from life and driving it back on itself, the impetus given by Left Wing politics is for the time exhausted, and however much we should like to have a paper that was revolutionary in opinions or original in technique, it is impossible to do so when there is a certain suspension of judgement and creative activity.

It is difficult to imagine a more glum manifesto. In the

absence of any of the impulses that normally give rise to new magazines, *Horizon* would, it appeared, content itself with providing writers with 'a place to express themselves' and readers with 'the best writing we can obtain'. Apart from that, its editor would sit tight and wait for developments, hoping that the present muddiness would give way to a situation clear enough for some kind of 'policy' to be envisaged:

> At the moment civilization is on the operating table and we sit in the waiting room. For so far this is a war without the two great emotions which made the Spanish conflict real to so many of us. It is a war which awakens neither Pity nor Hope, and what began as a routine police operation, a military sanction, is now hardening into the grim prehistorical necessity of Keeping Alive.

As to politics, the tone of the magazine was to be one of disappointed thirties leftism. Although 'our politics are in abeyance', both Connolly and Spender had been too involved in the literary movement of the last decade not to feel preoccupied with its demise. But this concern was to be far more evident in later issues than it was at first. Connolly was anxious to start out with at least the appearance of a clean sheet.

The first number carried poems by Auden, de la Mare, Betjeman and MacNeice, a story by H. E. Bates, a travel piece by Connolly himself, and two meditations on the war by Herbert Read and J. B. Priestley. The whole thing was exquisitely non-committal, exhibiting all the received names, the names that readers would have been used to seeing in any one of the several annuals and miscellanies that were appearing at the time. There was a literary-critical section, but it comprised no more than a few crisp shorter notices of new books – Connolly had warned in his editorial that *Horizon*'s criticism would carry either lengthy essays or brief notes. There would be 'no half-hearted comment on the half-dead'.

With the second issue Connolly was able to be slightly more precise in his puzzlement. He tended to prefer having his opinions extorted from him by the pressures of debate, and the magazine had now appeared, sold out and been widely attacked. *Horizon*, Connolly reports – almost with glee – had been derided as 'old-fashioned and Georgian', and its editorial had been 'escapist and cagy'. There was mockery too of his parading Priestley and Bates in his first issue; a similar magazine in the last war, it had been contended, would have been printing Joyce and Eliot. All this Connolly took in his stride, but it was significant that the one criticism which did seem to hit a nerve was in a *Reynolds's News* review which equated *Horizon*'s apparent opting out of political commitments with the departure to California of Auden and Isherwood ('to contemplate their navels'). Connolly's retort is oddly ambivalent, displaying a certain bitterness against the emigrants but also seeking to defend them. And he certainly does not rebut the analogy between their aloofness and *Horizon*'s. The writers' departure, in fact, is thought by him to be 'the most important literary event since the outbreak of the Spanish War':

> Auden is our best poet, Isherwood our most promising novelist. They did not suffer from lack of recognition in England where they received a publicity which they did everything to encourage, nor have they gone to America to animate the masses ... they are far-sighted and ambitious young men with a strong instinct of self-preservation, and an eye on the main chance, who have abandoned what they consider to be the sinking ship of European democracy, and by implication the aesthetic doctrine of social realism that has been prevailing here. Are they right? It would certainly seem so.

Auden's and Isherwood's abandonment of the doctrine of social realism (it is not doubted for a second that they supported such a doctrine) provides *Horizon* with the beginnings of its promised 'policy'. Puzzlement and inertia could pretend, at least for the time being, to have found a rationale. Social realism, Connolly maintains, could now be seen to have failed; it had 'set fire to a lot of rotten timber' but it had also damaged 'many green young saplings'. *Horizon* was not going to uphold discredited ideals of 'commitment' to the political arena. On the contrary, its job was to acknowledge the collapse of those ideals, and to attempt to reconstruct; to restate certain principles which the last decade had buried or abandoned – in particular, the (to social realists) most heretical principle of all: 'that writing as an art, is capable of producing a deep and satisfying emotion in the reader whether it is about Mozart, the fate of Austria, or the habits of bees'.

In the next few issues of *Horizon* there were repeated attempts to develop this point of view beyond mere assertion, but Connolly was never happy in the role of the pure aesthete. His disappointments had been too political. His real effort, as far as he could be said to have one, was to achieve 'a synthesis between the new aesthetic Twenties and the puritan Thirties'. But in the absence of any new writers who could be said to have even approached such a synthesis, he was still obliged to draw heavily, if gloomily, for his contributions from figures of the earlier decade. Poems by MacNeice, Spender and William Empson were prominent, but for a magazine that saw itself as chiefly a vehicle for imaginative writing there was a disturbing preponderance of literary-critical and political essays, many of them none too lively. The editorials, in fact, had to carry the weight of *Horizon*'s aestheticism, and here Connolly soon began demonstrating those frequent shifts of ground and heart which were almost to become the magazine's trademark.

In *Horizon*'s opening numbers, the war – though it was the subject of one or two articles, and of Spender's 'September Journal' – was more of a depressing backcloth than a centre-stage preoccupation, but Connolly was aware that he could not indefinitely maintain his air of lofty boredom. In the issue of May 1940 he turned his attention to the grim subject with evident reluctance, as if forced to leave more important matters to one side. Significantly, it was the war as 'the enemy of creative activity' that captured his interest; at the deepest level, he contended, the war had nothing to do with the arts, and the arts therefore need not have anything to do with the war. Connolly notes with satisfaction that very few of the thousand or so contributions received by the magazine had any direct bearing on the European conflict. This, he believes, is as it should be:

> ... writers and painters are wise and right to ignore it and to concentrate their talent on other subjects. Since they are politically impotent, they can use this time to develop at deeper emotional levels, or to improve their weapons by technical experiment, for they have so long been mobilized in various causes that they are losing the intellectual's greatest virtues: the desire to pursue the truth wherever it may lead, and the belief in the human mind as the supreme organ through which life can be apprehended, improved and intensified.

It sounds very pat; almost as if the war were a lucky break for artists (and, of course, intellectuals: Connolly was fond of equating the two breeds). But the editorial goes on somewhat perplexingly to remind readers of the obvious – that art is threatened by the war. Facism also presents a menace to 'liberty and security' (including those of artists) and the war, although not as anti-fascist as they could wish, is much more anti-fascist than anything else that has happened. So, although it is good not to write about the war, it is bad not to believe in it. In other words, whilst wishing to give voice to the irresponsibilities of his new aestheticism, Connolly is nervous of seeming acceptable to the pacifists. All in all, it could not have been easy for an artist of the time to have much idea of what advice he was being offered here.

Connolly's confusion about what attitude to strike towards the war was not to last much longer. The fall of France and the Blitz pretty well put paid to any remaining traces of bland isolationism, though he was never to lose the wish, at least, to find for the arts some gay, non-militarized zone. This wish was to induce some of his more striking about-turns. In response to a 'Letter from a Soldier' by Goronwy Rees (Rees had rather bitterly attacked Connolly's stand-offishness) he admits that on the whole *Horizon* has failed to take the war seriously and that it has lived 'in a state of euphoria to which the defensive situation gave rise'. But, euphoric or not, he was still forced to concede that in the end 'the labour of imagination', however autonomously superb, depended on the British fleet. 'Now that that extraordinary fact has been brought home to us,' he says, 'we cannot afford the airy detachment of earlier numbers.'

By December 1940 *Horizon* had settled into outright political support of the war effort, and to a vague and grudging acceptance of the necessity for writers and artists to cooperate in the defence of liberty. But he is by no means happy about the way the magazine's first year had gone and delivers the first of what were to become almost annual bouts of self-abasement. There were too few readers for a start. *Horizon*'s target was a circulation of ten thousand; 'after a year still half of them are hiding'. Connolly lists with some acrimony the reasons for this failure. First of all, there was the irritating unwillingness of big names to contribute: Eliot, Wells, Shaw, Forster, Virginia Woolf and so on had all been approached for work but had not responded. In their absence, *Horizon*'s contributors had been drawn from a rather narrower area than had been originally hoped. The magazine had tried to start 'with a clean record', with no distinction between highbrow and lowbrow, old or young, right or left, but that simply hadn't worked. The fact is, Connolly remarks, that whatever your egalitarian intentions, 'in the end you must rely for seventy per cent (of your contributors) on young socialist writers or left wing journalists and poets – and a sprinkling of pacifists; they are more lively, more prolific than any others'. The army, of course, hadn't helped; with heavy sarcasm, he recalls Goronwy Rees's criticism that *Horizon* ignored the experience of the writer in uniform and points out that writers in uniform had so far done nothing (in word or, in many cases, deed) to make them worth the magazine's notice. When a writer becomes 'a Warrior', his tendency is to stop writing. As to Rees himself:

> ... unless the dashing captain has now left these shores, it is he who is under the obligation to us for carrying on through the craters, and amid the looped and windowed raggedness of our offices, to provide him and his stern followers with something to read in their quarters in the West Country.

Sneers of this kind against the soldiery were to crop up time and again in *Horizon*. The magazine was to remain resolutely (if not unguiltily) an oasis of civilian values.

And the sneers were not just against the soldiery. The reading public as a whole, Connolly asserts, had panicked with the fall of France, and *Horizon*'s sales had fallen forty per cent as a result. 'It is with a certain bitterness that *Horizon* warns its public: "If we can go on producing a magazine in these conditions, the least you can do is read it." ' This note of paranoia, this suggestion that brave *Horizon* was doing everyone an unrewarded favour, was not without some justification. It *was* difficult to get the magazine out. There was the paper shortage, and the air raids. 'The offices of *Horizon* would seem to be a military objective second in importance only to our printers' and two thousand copies of the magazine had so far been destroyed by enemy action. The editors, though unpaid and likely to remain so, had all the same managed to keep production going and *Horizon* had yet to miss a month. It wasn't easy, and one can see how they might have felt aggrieved. But Connolly comes perilously close here (and at other times) to a whining self-righteousness which fits ill with his usual weary, offhand affectations.

In spite of such war-time grumbles, though, there was no longer any questioning of the war effort as a whole. Most of the original post-Spain snootiness was now aban-) doned, and Connolly closes his anniversary editorial with a stirring retort to those who had sneered at him for the 'glib cartwheels' which had brought him to his present patriotism:

> The fact is ... Churchill saved England from defeat more signally than any one man in history ... even if we owe nothing to Churchill but his oratory, we owe him everything. He saved us from panic when the real ingredients of panic were there.

Although *Horizon*'s fluctuating editorial moods were always entertaining, they didn't do much to vary the magazine's actual contents. There were strong issues (No. 13, for instance, carried Alun Lewis's 'All Day it has Rained', Louis MacNeice's 'Plurality' and Dylan Thomas's 'Deaths and Entrances') and there was a generally high level of intelligence throughout. But there was no clear sense of direction, of the magazine being able (or even, as far as anyone could tell, willing) to provide more than just a place to print things. And the contemporary audience was not as indulgent towards Connolly's whims as we, looking back, might be. In No. 16, for instance, the results of a questionnaire sent out to readers showed that 'indecision, inconsistency, waveringness' were high on the list of accusations. Connolly's bland response was surely blander than he must have felt: 'Our doubt is our passion, and our passion is our task':

> Being interested in the truth (*Horizon*) can neither express the bluff certainties of the fighting man, nor the irrespon-

sibilities of those who are convinced the war is not worth fighting nor take refuge, as do so many intellectuals, in putting their certainties into the future, when the war is over.

It was probably no accident that, in the very next issue, Connolly followed up this piece of haughtiness with an editorial that seems to have been deliberately designed to outrage his solemn readership's demands. He gives a report on a spring evening stroll through the bombed-out areas of London. The man of sensibility is seen inspecting the damage in Bayswater and Kensington and in Leicester Square. Such is his super-fastidiousness that he is able to feel 'no pity for the fate of such houses'. Their architecture was so bad they *deserved* to be bombed. But when Connolly gets to Chelsea, it's a different story:

> Chelsea in the milky green evening light, where the church where Henry James was buried is a pile of red rubble, where the late eighteenth century houses gape with their insides blown out, like ruined triumphal arches, is a more tragic spectacle. For here the life that has vanished with the buildings that once housed it was of some consequence; there was some fine appreciation of books and pictures, and many calm hideouts for the people who made them. It was one of the last strongholds of the cultivated haute bourgeoisie where leisure, however ill-earned, was seldom more agreeably made use of. Now when the sun shines on these sandy ruins and on the brown and blue men working there one expects to see goats, and a goatherd in a burnous – sirenes in delubris voluptatis – pattering among them.

Apart from the awesome snobbery, there is the simple (and some might think brutal) absurdity of this fantasy which Connolly seems not to notice. It was when this side of the editorial presence was most nakedly in evidence that

Horizon's smooth, untroubled maintenance of the old values began to look not brave but blind.

In the same issue, Connolly contrives to make things look even worse by engaging in a gratuitous attack on Joyce and Proust; the limpid aesthete denigrates both as 'very sick men, great invalids who, in spite of enormous talent, were crippled by the same disease – Elephantiasis of the ego'. Such harsh judgements were not often heard in *Horizon*, and it is entirely typical that on this occasion Connolly should lose his nerve, let his wrists slacken, and slump once more into comfortable elegiacs:

> Yet we must remember that the life many of us are now leading is inimical to the appreciation of literature . . . It is as unfair to judge art in these philistine conditions as if we were seasick.

This plangently valetudinarian note was to become a regular feature of *Horizon* and was perhaps its truest, most consistent voice, though it usually managed to stiffen up into at least the appearance of purpose and conviction. To take a typical mood-chart. In October 1941 we find Connolly appealing, along with a number of other writers (including Orwell, Koestler, Spender and Alun Lewis) for the formation of an official group of war writers. If there were war painters, it was challengingly grumbled, why were there not equally official artists who could paint the war in words? All very purposeful. But by May 1942 Connolly is back in the dumps, expressing utter weariness with boring talk about the 'role and responsibility of the artist'. His new demand is for

> a moratorium on Art till the war is over. All writers who feel that they are in the war and responsible for winning it should be excused literary activity, and even forbidden it.

Instead of writing, writers should spend their spare time reading. 'The war,' sighed the editor of one of England's two leading war-time literary magazines, 'is not conducive to good writing – that can wait till afterwards,' No sooner, though, had *Horizon*'s readers got this uncheering prospect settled in their minds than Connolly perks up, and again dives into the deeps of idealistic fervour. In July 1942 he declares that '*Horizon* is a literary magazine . . . our role (in relation to national disasters) is to play our instrument a little louder and a little better, like a ship's orchestra, as our vessel blunders from rock to rock. Artists,' he continues, *do* have a job in war-time; they must continue to produce art which will make 'our culture into something worth fighting for'. Maybe, many a reader must have concluded, it all depended on the weather.

Needless to say, Connolly's attitude to the quality of his magazine was as fickle as his understanding of its functions. At one moment he will be found exhorting readers to contribute to *Horizon*'s Begging Bowl, and heatedly reaffirming the magazine's crucial excellence. But gloom was far more often the order of the day, and Connolly was frequently to be found wondering if the whole thing was really in the least worth-while. In October 1942 he complains that now that *Horizon* has become an established institution, it is getting to seem atrophied. Superficially all was well with the magazine – paper trickles in, exports increase, subscribers renew 'and the genteel deficit expected from a literary magazine is maintained without a vulgar lapse into profit or a disastrous cascade into loss'. But what about the contents? Because the war had scattered the community of writers, the age of his contributors had been steadily rising (in evidence of this he rather insultingly points to two contributions in the current number by Laurence Binyon (seventy) and Logan Pearsall Smith (seventy-seven). But in any case, it is not at all clear that even if the younger writers weren't scattered they would have anything much to contribute:

> Such movements of young writers as we have started since the war seem to be more conspicuous for the violence of

their attacking power than the depth of their emotions, and to include their efforts would be to remove that emphasis on performance rather than on promise which it has been the policy of *Horizon* to keep up.

In the 1942 Christmas issue this morose note is amplified into a richer gloom; indeed, into a death-warrant. *Horizon*, it is announced, is three years and thirty-six numbers old. 'Too old in fact':

> Think how ridiculous *Horizon* will look (after the war) – no manifesto, no movements, a magazine which to defeat the call-up has learnt to appear without writers, which can see only in the blackout, which can comment only on disaster, or maintain itself in a paper shortage.

Fifty numbers, Connolly predicts, should be the maximum for a magazine with so few natural advantages. *Horizon* will by then be older than the *Yellow Book*, older than *Transition*. It will be ready for a beautiful demise:

> And at fifty, not to die, but to commit suicide – to publish one number in which everybody said what they really thought and then be suppressed. Suppression is the deep unconscious goal of every magazine, its secret death-wish . . .

Suppression may have been Cyril Connolly's secret fantasy, but he was right in believing that little that had appeared in *Horizon* during its first three years had been in the least likely to tempt such an interesting fate. There had been good poems, but these had grown fewer and fewer, some excellent essays (among them Orwell's 'Boys' Weeklies' and 'The Art of Donald MacGill') but all in all the prose contributions had become stodgy and predictable. There had been hardly any short stories of merit. A few lumps of Mass Observation, some autobiography from Spender and Augustus John, two essays by Clement Greenberg reprinted from the *Partisan Review*: these, along with the Orwell, had helped to vary the diet, but *Horizon*'s chief dependence was on the lengthy, reappraising critical study of literary figures of the past: Lawrence, Proust, Barrie. These tended to be polite, worthy and dull. There was very little from America and not much more from Europe, in spite of Connolly's traveloguish sighs in that direction, and a general weakness for essays on French writers of the nineteenth century.

The fourth year, which brought *Horizon* perilously close to its predicted suicide, was in fact much as before, though Connolly did show signs of wishing to introduce more war reportage into the magazine. A comparison with John Lehmann's *New Writing* shows how half-hearted that wish really was. Indeed, such a comparison demonstrates how extraordinarily little *Horizon* did manage to say about the war in forms other than the opinionating essay or editorial.

The magazine's forty-ninth issue appeared in January 1944, but far from planning any funerals Connolly found himself pleading with his contributors for more effort, more variety of content, in the future. And the fiftieth number showed that *Horizon*'s death-wish, though as vigorous as ever, was nowhere near consummation. The editor contented himself with obituary:

> What have we lost or gained intellectually by five years of war? We have gained in seriousness, but lost in mental elasticity; the emotional strain of war has broken our curiosity, has fatigued us to the point at which we are cynical, impervious, distressed or hostile in the presence of new ideas.

With the approach of peace, it was difficult to keep up this high standard of world-weariness, and indeed there is suddenly a bizarre surge of optimism throughout the magazine as Connolly contemplates the possibility of once more being able to take his holidays abroad. 'We shall return,' he enthused, 'to Europe to draw strength from the continent we have set free until the full tide of our Western civilization flows back over the scattered dried-up rock pools that every nation has become, to set them all breathing and moving again in the cool element of which they have so long been deprived.' In preparation for this glad renaissance, Connolly inaugurates a series of travelogues under the title, 'Where Shall Johnny Go' – Johnny being the civilized young Englishman anxious to equip himself for post-war tourism. Connolly's own delight at the prospect of such pleasures even leads him to write an open letter to the soldiery, envying the fighting man the opportunity he has had of fulfilling a heroic, historical role, and also the chances he has had to see the world, to have adventures and to win applause. It is an extraordinary outburst in many ways, but it sheds light on the general shiftiness of *Horizon*'s war-time stance:

> Of course all the time you had to fight. Don't think I am unaware of all this fighting, it is just that which churns the guilt round and round till it curdles into a kind of rancorous despair. You were always fighting for me, in the favoured places of the world, and writing me your friendly unpatronizing letters which I have to answer. Oh, why can't I fight for myself?
>
> Never in the whole war has the lot of the civilian been more abject, or his status so low – he is the unpopular schoolboy in the keen, tough school whose fees are ten shillings in the pound, with no one who will take him in for the holidays. Meanwhile, what about you Victor? Fighting as usual, making history, drinking calvados . . .

The schoolboy analogy, though breathtaking in its inadequacy, does fit with the tone of the whole letter, which is sulking, petulant and egocentric. Connolly had had five years of war in which to air such feelings, but he only chooses to do so when peace is just around the corner, when fighting really can be thought of with envy as having all to do with glory and good drink. During the war, the magazine's attitude to 'the warrior' was never more than grudging and very often it was straightforwardly patronizing. But, of course, those were the years in which, as Stephen Spender has recorded, soldiers bought the magazine because it offered *them* something to envy.

With its fifth anniversary issue (December 1944) *Horizon* offers the usual groans about 'the general deterioration of humanity', and there is also a 'final' declaration of the magazine's policy, as if by now everyone hadn't worked it out for himself:

> By now we should have a policy. We have. Accused of 'aestheticism', 'escapism', 'ivory towerism', 'bourgeois formalism', 'frivolity' and 'preferring art to life', it pleads on all these counts 'guilty and proud of it'.

The prospect of a soon-to-be-visitable France enables him to indulge in a new surge of literary Francophilia at the expense of the 'anarchic sulking' which he claims is the English writer's current posture. In France there has been the advantage of 'fraternal conspiracy against the aggressor' – this comradeship had enabled the French writer to stay fresh and ideological (to be like, it is interestingly contended, the English writer during the Spanish conflict). 'They have been hungry, but they have not been worn out by long hours, air-raids and propaganda work.' Again, one is amazed by the casual cheapening of the soldier-writer's lot (and, incidentally, of the French resistance writer's; *he* didn't have long hours and was altogether innocent, it seemed, of the terrors of propaganda work). In January 1945, Connolly was able to get to France at last, to see it all for himself. His reaction was as might have been expected; an easy elevation of the foreign virtues used to slander the domestic scene:

London seemed utterly remote – a grey, sick wilderness on another planet, for in Paris the civilian virtues triumph – personal relations, adultminded seriousness, aliveness, love of the arts. Literature is enormously important there and one sees how pervasive, though impalpable, have become the irritable lassitude, brain-fatigue, apathy and hum-drummery of English writers.

In May 1945 a French number of *Horizon* appeared, with contributions from Sartre, Valéry and Ponge, pieces by Stephen Spender on French poetry and by Philip Toynbee on the general literary scene. All, it was complacently implied, was well again.

In fact, of course, it wasn't, and Connolly's initial burst of peace-time euphoria was soon to fade. By September 1945 it had become clear that there was going to be a long labour of reconstruction in Europe before men of taste could resume their customary habits. After its rosy summer, *Horizon* was once more languishing in the lowest of low spirits. 'The great marquee of European civilization ... has fallen down.' France, after all, had deteriorated and was exhibiting signs of 'moral apathy, the physical slowness of recovery'. And as for Britain:

> ... what a winter this is going to be in this most favoured of European countries – no coal, though the earth is stiff with it; no wine, though the cellars of Bordeaux are full; no servants, though there are millions of displaced personages who would be only too glad to find places; no trips abroad, no access to snow or sun; only art and a little politics to keep us warm by.

Yes, it was going to be tough. Gloomy articles from Berlin and Cologne, however, made it clear that it was going to be far tougher elsewhere, and by May 1946 Connolly was beginning to regret those European ecstasies. He had been on a trip to Switzerland, where he had – for some private reason –

been preparing a Swiss number of the magazine:

> If there is one sentiment which we have tried to avoid in *Horizon*, it is national pride. But returning after six weeks I felt from Dover to London what can only be described as a patriotic glow. First, because we have no black market with its consequent atmosphere of dishonesty and an immense cleavage between the rich and poor. Next, because the new cocktail bar on the Golden Arrow is a cheerful and ingenious affirmation of the right to pleasure, something which is post-war and not merely a return to pre-war, a lyric contribution to the poetry of motion.

It is remarkable how often Connolly's attitudes were determined by the simple matter of where the food and drink was to be found.

Neither, of course, were easy to come by in 1946 and a repeated theme in *Horizon* during this and the following year was to be the theme of money. One of the magazine's preoccupations from the start had been 'the situation of the artist' (usually meaning his financial situation) and there had been odd editorial rumblings about the need for some kind of state patronage. This plea became more explicit as the age of austerity settled into its crippled stride. A questionnaire was sent out in 1946 to contributors to *Horizon*, asking each of them 'How much do you think a writer needs to live on?' The writers' demands turned out to vary quite a lot, ranging from £500 a year (George Orwell, Alex Comfort), through £1000 (Stephen Spender, V. S. Pritchett) up to as much as £3,500 (Elizabeth Bowen). Connolly himself considered five pounds per day to be sufficient for the writer 'if he is to enjoy leisure and privacy, buy books, travel and entertain his friends'. On the other hand, of course, 'if he is prepared to die young of syphilis for the sake of an adjective he can make do on under'.

It is not surprising that with cash so short, *Horizon* began turning its gaze (along with the rest of Europe) to America.

There had been very little American representation in the magazine up to this point – indeed, what there had been had mainly comprised reprints from *Partisan Review* – and the general attitude to trans-Atlantic culture had been fairly patronizing. By February 1947, though, readers began hearing of the 'vain, confident, affable and aggressive' Yanks, whose energy made the British seem so pallid and played-out:

> ... most of us are not men or women but members of a vast, seedy, over-worked, over-legislated, neuter class, with our drab clothes, our ration books and murder stories, our envious, stricken, old-world apathies and resentments – a careworn people.

The plaint ends with a demand for writers to be liberated from this drabness by state patronage: 'Art is not a necessity but an indispensable luxury; those who produce it must be cosseted.' In America, of course, they ordered these things better, and by October 1947 *Horizon*'s capitulation to the New World was complete. A double number on the 'Arts in America' appeared; the weary Europeans handing on the torch to the thrusting young:

> As Europe becomes more helpless the Americans are forced to become far-seeing and responsible, as Rome was forced by the long decline of Greece to produce an Augustus, a Vergil. *Our impotence liberates their potentialities*. Something important is about to happen, as if the wonderful *jeunesse* of America were suddenly to retain their idealism and vitality and courage and imagination into adult life, and become the wise and good who make use of them.

The issue itself was something of a rag-bag. It had the expected *Partisan Review* contingent, some poems by Marianne Moore, Wallace Stevens and E. E. Cummings, John Berryman's 'The Imaginary Jew', and a piece on American advertising by someone called Herbert Marshall McLuhan. Most readers will, one imagines, have found a discrepancy between the rousing purposefulness of the editorial and the obvious randomness of the actual contributions. But with *Horizon* they were used to that.

Horizon, as we have seen, had had its low moments before, but the American issue represented a new level of weariness; *Horizon* might, in its Anglophobic moods, have been able to envisage a future for itself as a European magazine. It could hardly forge ahead, though, as an outpost of America. The end really was in sight this time. During the last two years of the magazine's life, it simply ticked over – Connolly made very infrequent editorial appearances and apart from a flurry of excitement over a very successful special number entirely devoted to Evelyn Waugh's *The Loved One* (February 1948) its usual performance was mechanical and wan. Even the old miseries seemed to have evaporated. The hundredth number came and went, with barely a passing grumble: *Horizon*, it recorded, had been the witness of a steady decline in all the arts. It had seen the collapse of the cultivated bourgeoisie who used to make it possible for good art to be made, and now it observed on all sides the ruin of promising talents: 'Every writer I know under sixty (except one or two prosperous novelists) is ruining his talent through hack-work and part-time jobs'. There was no longer any suggestion that a magazine like *Horizon* could in any way help to mend the situation.

Horizon managed a further nineteen numbers before announcing, in November 1949, that the next issue would 'commemorate the tenth year of our existence, after which the magazine will close down for a year and reopen, if conditions improve, in an invigorated form for Xmas, 1950.' The magazine's premises in Bedford Square had to be vacated, it was explained; but it was also made clear that this was no more than a timely pretext. *Horizon*'s circulation had remained static for years, while printing costs had rocketed.

Only American sales had kept it going, and there seemed no chance of securing the thousand new subscribers who would ensure a temporary solvency. And in any case 'A decade of our lives is quite enough to devote to a lost cause such as the pursuit and marketing of quality in contemporary writing'. Therefore, *Horizon* would not be sorry to retire

> ... into the long-desired shade, to the satisfaction of the envious, the distress of our friends and the indifference of all but that one in every one hundred and fifty thousand who constitute our world public.

'The long-desired shade.' Certainly, no other magazine had flaunted its death-wish quite so openly or so energetically. It is entirely fitting that of all Connolly's editorials the one he is now most remembered by should be his last. A man who so loved the terminal could hardly have failed to take advantage of such an exquisite opportunity for immortality:

> One can perceive the inner trend of the Forties as maintaining this desperate struggle of the modern movement, between man, betrayed by science, bereft of religion, deserted by the pleasant imaginings of humanism against the blind fate of which he is now so expertly conscious that if we were to close this last Comment with the suggestion that everyone who now is reading it may in ten years time, or even five, look back to this moment as the happiest in their lives, there would be few who would gainsay us. 'Nothing dreadful is ever done with, no bad thing gets any better; you can't be too serious.' This is the message of the Forties from which, alas, there seems no escape, for it is closing time in the gardens of the West and from now on an artist will be judged only by the resonance of his solitude or the quality of his despair.

It is doubtful that many readers *did* look back on December 1949 as the happiest moment in their lives, but there can be little doubt that *Horizon* had rarely been more cheerful. Its glum, muddled, endearing flirtation with apocalypse had reached its consummation. On balance, literature must be grateful that it took so long.

Index

Abel, Lionel, 112
Adelphi, The, 92
Agee, James, 112
Aldington, Richard, 17, 49, 52, 54
Allott, Kenneth, 78, 93, 97
Anderson, Margaret, 11-43, 65
Anderson, Sherwood, 12
Angel Island, 15
Antheil, Georgette, 40
Anvil, The, 108
Arnold, Matthew, 68
Ashleigh, Charles, 17
Auden, W. H., 78, 81, 84, 86, 87, 98, 126, 127, 128

Barker, George, 78, 86, 90, 91
Barrie, James, 138
Barry, Iris, 26, 32
Bates, H. E., 127, 128
Baudelaire, Charles, 50
Beechcroft, T. O., 78
Bergson, Henri, 13
Berryman, John, 143
Best Poems of the Year, 84

Betjeman, John, 127
Binyon, Lawrence, 136
Blast, 8, 18, 25, 56, 83
Blunden, Edmund, 94
Bodenheim, Maxwell, 17, 25, 38
Boldero, Martin, 92
Bottrall, Ronald, 87
Bowen, Elizabeth, 142
Box of God, The, 64
Bradley, Andrew Cecil, 68
Brancusi, 41
Breton, André, 116
Bridge, The, 79
Brooke, Rupert, 13, 16, 18, 57, 63

Cameron, Norman, 86, 87
Campbell, Roy, 94
Cantleman's Spring Mate, 26, 29
Cantos' 89
Carnevali, Emmanuel, 61, 62
Carter, Huntly, 20
Chamberlain, John, 118
Chatfield-Taylor, Hobart C., 45
Chicago, 12, 16, 21, 59

INDEX 149

Chicago, 53, 63
Churchill, Sir Winston, 133
Cocteau, Jean, 41, 78
Comfort, Alex, 142
Conkling, Grace Howard, 47
Connolly, Cyril, 126-46
Conroy, Jack, 101
Contempary Poetry and Prose, 8
Contemporania, 52, 63
Continent, 12
Cowley, Malcolm, 104
Crane, Hart, 78, 79
Criterion, The, 67-80
Criticism of Poetry, The, 85
Cromwell, Gladys, 58
Cummings, E. E., 143

Dadaism, 37
Dark Flower, The, 13
Day Lewis, C., 84, 88, 96, 97, 98, 105
De Coursey Patterson, Antoinette, 58
De Gourmont, Remy, 32, 35
De la Mare, Walter, 127
Dell, Floyd, 12
Des Imagistes, 17
Disinherited, The, 101
Dog Beneath the Skin, 93
Doone, Rupert, 93
Dreiser, Theodore, 12
Dupee, F. W., 109

East Coker, 120
Eeldrop and Appleplex, 25
Egoist, The, 56
Eliot, T. S., 24, 25, 26, 32, 34, 55, 56, 64, 67-80, 102, 104, 120, 128, 131
Empson, William, 78, 129
English Review, The, 60
Everyman, 92
Exile's Return, 104

Faber and Gwyer, 71
Farrell, James T., 101, 112, 118

Faust, 14
Ficke, Arthur Davison, 12, 13
First Poems, 91
Flaubert, Gustave, 51, 112
Fletcher, John Gould, 73, 78
Flint, F. S., 52
Form in Modern Poetry, 89
Forster, E. M., 131
Fortune, 109
Foster, George Burman, 14
France, Anatole, 75
Franco, General, 112
Frazer, Sir James, 73
Freeman, Joseph, 104
Frost, Robert, 34, 63

Gains, Ruth, 58
Galsworthy, John, 12, 13, 18
Garnett, Louise Ayre, 58
Gascoyne, David, 86
Gautier, Théophile, 51
General William Booth Enters into Heaven, 53, 63
Giacometti, 86
Gide, André, 75, 112
Gilmore, Inez Haynes, 15
Goldman, Emma, 15, 16, 17, 19, 42
Good Housekeeping, 12
Greenberg, Clement, 99, 120, 121, 122, 138
Greenwood, Julia Wickham, 58
Gregory, Allene, 58
Grigson, Geoffrey, 78, 81-98, 126
Gryphon, The, 92

Hamilton, Norah Rowan, 65
Hayes, Alfred, 105
Heap, Jane, 22, 23, 24, 28, 30-40, 42
'H. D.', 17, 50, 52
Hemingway, Ernest, 82
Henderson, Alice Corbin, 49
Heppenstall, Rayner, 91, 92
Hicks, Granville, 101, 107

150 INDEX

Hillstrom, Joe, 20
Hitler, Adolf, 76
Hook, Sidney, 122
Horizon, 125-46
Hound and Horn, 79
Huebsch, 29

Imaginary Letters, 25
Imagism, 19, 51, 52, 77
Imagist Anthology, 78
Isherwood, Christopher, 93, 97, 128

Jackson, Elmer, 101
James, Henry, 32, 35
Jepson, Edgar, 34, 59
Jodinranath Mawhor's Occupation, 25
John, Augustus, 138
John Reed Club, 99, 100, 103, 107
Jolas, Eugene, 115
Jones, Llewellyn, 14
Joyce, James, 24, 29, 31, 42, 128, 135

Kenyon Review, 123
Kilmer, Joyce, 63
Kipling, Rudyard, 51
Koestler, Arthur, 135
Kora in Hell, 34, 38

Lawrence, D. H., 58, 138
Leavis, F., 85, 89
Leblanc, Georgette, 40, 41
Lehmann, John, 138
Lewis, Alun, 133, 135
Lewis, Wyndham, 8, 26, 27, 82, 89
Lindsay, Vachel, 34, 53, 54, 56, 64
Listener, The, 88, 92
Little Review, The, 7, 11-43, 56, 59, 65
London Mercury, 82
Long, Lily A., 49
Lorimer, Emilia Stuart, 47
Lowell, Amy, 16, 18
Lucas, F. L., 85

MacDiarmid, Hugh, 94
MacDonald, Dwight, 109, 115, 116, 120, 121, 122, 123, 124
MacDowell, Gerty, 30
MacLeish, Archibald, 104
MacNeice, Louis, 87, 97, 127, 129, 133
Madge, Charles, 78, 86
Madox Hueffer, Ford, 50, 51
Making It, 99
March Review, The, 12
Masefield, John, 14, 51
Mason and Hamlin Company, 16
Mass Observation, 94-5
Masters, Lee, 34
Maurras, Charles, 68, 74
McCarthy, Mary, 109
McLuhan, Herbert Marshall, 144
Mew, Charlotte, 63
Meynell, Alice, 14
Monro, Harold, 78
Monroe, Harriet, 34, 44, 45-66
Monthly Criterion, The, 72
Moore, Marianne, 42, 63, 143
Morley, Frank, 71
Morning Post, The, 82
Morris, George L. K., 109
Mosley, Oswald, 73
Muir, Edwin, 97

New Bearings, 89
New Country, 84
New Criterion, The, 72
New English Weekly, The, 92
New Masses, 109, 114, 118
New Republic, 118
New Verse, 81-98, 125, 126
New Writing, 138
New York Society for the Prevention of Vice, 29
New York World, 48
New Yorker, 112
Newhouse, Edward, 104

INDEX 151

Newman, Cardinal, 68
Nietzsche, Friedrich, 13, 14, 15, 18, 19, 75

Oliver, Frederick Scott, 71
Oliver, Garcia, 116
One Way Song, 87
Orwell, George, 122, 135, 137, 142

Paid on Both Sides, 78
Partisan Review, 9, 99-124, 138, 143
Pavannes and Divisions, 61
Pearsall Smith, Logan, 136
Phelps, Wallace, 102, 103, 104, 106
Phillips, William, 108, 109, 123
Picasso, Pablo, 112
Podhoretz, Norman, 99
Poe, Edgar Allan, 50
Poetry, 9, 17, 24, 34, 36, 44-66
Ponge, Francis, 141
Pound, Ezra, 17, 23, 25, 26, 28, 29, 32, 33, 35, 39, 41, 45-66, 79, 89
Powys, J. C., 12
Priestley, J. B., 127, 128
Pritchett, V. S., 142
Proust, Marcel, 78, 135, 138
Prufrock, 26, 55, 56, 78
Pudney, John, 87

Quinn, John, 24, 27, 28, 29, 30, 31, 32, 69, 70

Rahv, Philip, 99, 100, 102, 103, 104, 106, 109, 112, 113, 118, 119, 120, 121, 122, 123
Read, Herbert, 68, 82, 89, 97, 127
Reader Critic, The, 15, 25
Rees, Goronwy, 131, 132
Reynolds's News, 128
Richmond, Bruce, 71
Ridge, Lola, 58
Ripostes, 112

Roberts, Michael, 84, 85, 94
Robinson, Eloise, 58
Rock, The, 90
Rodker, John, 26, 32, 35, 39
Rolfe, Edwin, 107
Romains, Jules, 35
Rosenberg, Isaac, 57
Rothermere, Viscountess, 69, 71
Roughton, Roger, 8

Sandburg, Carl, 53, 56, 61, 64
Sarett, Lew, 60-1, 64, 65
Sartre, Jean-Paul, 14
Schwartz, Delmore, 112
Scrutiny, 85, 87
Seagull, The, 12
Second Hymn to Lenin, 94
Shanks, Edward, 18
Shaw, Bernard, 131
Silone, 112
Sitwell, Edith, 42, 83, 88
Skinner, Constance Lindsay, 56
Solow, Herbert, 114
Some Imagist Poets, 19
Southern Review, 123
Spectator, The, 88
Spender, Stephen, 78, 84, 85, 86, 87, 88, 90, 97, 120, 126, 127, 129, 135, 138, 140, 141, 142
Stalin, Joseph, 116, 117
Stevens, Wallace, 60, 63, 94, 95, 112, 143
St. Vincent Millay, Edna, 60, 63
Story of a Round House, The, 51
Strobel, Marion, 63
Sumner, John, 29, 30
Surrealism, 86
Swinburne, Algernon C., 51
Swingler, Randall, 87
Symons, Julian, 80

Tagore, Rabindranath, 53, 54

Tate, Allen, 85, 87
Tessimond, A. S. J., 87
Thomas, Dylan, 90, 133
Tietjens, Eunice, 16, 18
The Loved One, 144
The Magnetic Mountain, 105
Times Literary Supplement, 71
Toynbee, Philip, 141
Transition, 115, 137
Tribune (Chicago), 44
Trotsky, Leo, 119
Twenty-Seven Sonnets, 98
Tzara, 41

Ulysses, 29, 30, 31, 32, 39, 43
Upward, Edward, 84

Valéry, Paul, 78, 141
Verlaine, Paul, 19
Vienna, 90
Von Freytag-Loringhoven, Baroness Else, 36-9

Waste Land, The, 64, 78, 79
Waugh, Evelyn, 144

Wells, H. G., 131
Whibley, Charles, 71
Whitman, Walt, 50
Widdemer, Margaret, 49
Wagner, Richard, 18
War Sonnets, 57
Wilde, Oscar, 19
Williams, William Carlos, 34, 37, 38, 63, 64, 78
Wilson, Edmund, 112
Wing, De Witt C., 12, 14, 16
Winters, Yvor, 63
Wolfe, Humbert, 78
Woolf, Virginia, 131
Wright, Frank Lloyd, 16
Wyatt, Edith, 51

Year's Poetry, The, 88, 97
Yeats, W. B., 40, 49, 50, 53, 54, 56, 60
Yellow Book, 137
Young Manhood of Studs Lonigan, The, 102
Youth, 73

Zarathustra, 15